FLIP IT LIKE THIS!

DAVID HAYWARD
THE ARTIST BEHIND @NAKEDPASTOR

Broadleaf Books

Minneapolis

FLIP IT LIKE THIS!

Cover design: 1517 Media

Print ISBN: 978-1-5064-8472-3
eBook ISBN: 978-1-5064-8473-0

Printed in Canada

Praise for *Flip It Like This!*

"David Hayward's work has touched my soul, personally. *Flip It Like This!* is a beautiful exploration of deconstructing your conditioned beliefs to become more open, compassionate, and heart-centered. Religious trauma is very real, and Hayward is a pioneer of bringing people back to the truth of themselves. I recommend this book to anyone on their own healing journey."

—**Dr. Nicole Lepera**, The Holistic Psychologist and author of *How to Do the Work*

"Thank God for David Hayward! For as long as I've been on the internet, Hayward's @nakedpastor cartoons have encouraged me, given me hope, and kicked me in my religious ass more times than I can count. But that's why I love him—his prophetic critique of the modern church is consistent, sharp-witted, and always on point. This collection of Hayward's funny, often poignant takes on evangelical churchisms is like a new chapter of the Book of Psalms—thoughtful reflections of God's truest heart."

—**Matthew Paul Turner**, #1 *New York Times* bestselling author

"David Hayward's cartoons don't shy away from tackling many of the ways in which Christianity has caused trauma for different people. Hayward's clever comics make those of us asking questions of our faith and grappling with religious abuse feel less alone and more understood."

—**Jo Luehmann**, writer

"You won't find a more loving, or on point, critique of institutional Christianity than this collection of cartoons from @NakedPastor. Some will induce guffaws, and some a wry chuckle, but all of them add up to a wonderfully meaningful commentary on questions of faith, individualism, and inclusivity!"

—**Bruce Cockburn**, singer and songwriter

"The gift of an artist and a cartoonist is not to placate the audience but to compassionately confront, to poke, and prod into discomfort, and encourage and affirm when you thought no one was listening or even aware. David Hayward is a gift."

—**Wm. Paul Young**, author of *The Shack and Lies We Believe about God*

"David Hayward's illustrated depictions of some of the most harmful aspects of the church are so poignantly accurate. You can't help but pause and reflect on the historical roots of white supremacy and the ill-conceived ideologies and practices that it's created in spaces of faith. His cartoons help me envision faith through a lens of love, hope, and change!"

—**Alma Zaragoza-Petty**, social justice advocate and author
of *Chingona: Owning Your Inner Badass for Healing and Justice*

"*Flip It Like This!* cuts to the chase of the church's dysfunction with the knife of prophetic vision. The charming rainbow sheep so many of us have come to love, along with other characters in David Hayward's comic imagination, wander through the pages of this collection, inviting us to see belonging, faith, morality, and justice like we've never viewed them before. Anyone who has both loved and been harmed by the church needs this book."

—**Jonathan Merritt**, contributing writer for *The Atlantic* and author of *Learning to Speak God from Scratch*

"The cartoons in *Flip It Like This!* are so apt that you might think David Hayward has been peeking through the windows of your church—or chatting with folks slipping out the back door. In Hayward's cartoons, that's where Jesus is standing anyway: outside, beside the outcasts and castoffs. With tender vision and withering wit, Hayward exposes hypocrisy and calls us to account. This delightful collection is chock full of irreverent grace, which may just save us all."

—**Kirsten Powers**, *New York Times* bestselling author of *Saving Grace*,
CNN senior political analyst, and *USA Today* columnist

"I have been a fan for a decade, ever since I sat with a friend and went through Hayward's Nakedpastor 101. We laughed to the point of tears as we saw the church world in which we had been oriented. I have often included Hayward's cartoons in my presentations because they so often speak more than a thousand sermons. People worldwide are finding that they are ready to stop waiting for a seat at a table they should have flipped long ago. *Flip It Like This!* may be Hayward's magnum opus."

—**Rev. Dr. David Moore**, activist and pastor

"David Hayward's work continues to put form to questions and feelings I've had but haven't always known now to articulate. Could life and love be bigger, more beautiful, and more available to everyone than we realized? When I encounter Hayward's work, I always sense the answer to this question is a resounding yes."

—**Jon Steingard**, host of *The Wonder* and The Mystery of Being podcast

"David Hayward's cartoons are peculiarly poignant in their critique of conservative Christians' rigidity and lack of compassion. *Flip it Like This!* made me, as a queer exvangelical, both laugh and cry, and I suspect that anyone who has felt alienated while sitting in evangelical pews will find a similar emotional resonance in these pages. Hayward has been there, and he gets it."

—**Chrissy Stroop**, senior correspondent for *Religion Dispatches* and
coeditor of *Empty the Pews: Stories of Leaving the Church*

PREFACE

I've always loved a good cartoon, preferably in one frame. I drew my first cartoon in September 2006 as an experiment—another cartoonist inspired me to start conveying my thoughts and feelings through cartoons, so I challenged myself to draw one every day until I ran out of ideas. I gave myself a month or so.

Fifteen years later, I'm still at it. I've drawn literally thousands of cartoons by now. You are holding in your hands the top 125 NakedPastor cartoons: my first "best of" collection.

Viewers' responses to my work have ranged from enraged to validated to enlightened and everything in between. Those are pretty powerful emotional responses—deep, sustained reactions my writing alone would never get. Frankly, I didn't expect my cartoons would be so polarizing. But affirmation, acceptance, inclusion, and love have always been offensive to some people, especially those who consider themselves the gatekeepers of who's in and who's out, who belongs and who doesn't, who meets the criteria and who doesn't. Alas, it seems things haven't changed much in that regard since I began drawing. But I will keep cartooning, because the cartoons seem to be doing something good. I love their direct, effective, and rapid way of communicating what I believe to be true.

A picture is worth a thousand sermons. You can scroll past a sermon, close your ears, zone out, ignore, and delete. But one-frame cartoons—good ones, at least, as hopefully a few of mine are—plow past our defenses and strike straight to the heart. And you can't unsee them.

I want to offer a caveat or two. When I draw a cartoon of "God," well, the concept of God is inconceivable! So I choose to go with the traditional trope: the old white guy with a beard in the sky. Of course I do not envision God like that. But this is the kind of illusion I hope to challenge, by using the illusion itself to hold a mirror up to its own deficiencies. It's the same with Jesus. A man of his time and place would be darker skinned. Jesus is often portrayed as a person of color in my cartoons, but in plain black-and-white line drawings, there is no color. Just lines.

In *Flip It Like This!*, my hope is that art, like action, speaks louder than words. I hope the image of Jesus showing a woman how to flip a table sticks with you. Art is like that. As opposed to words, which can more easily bounce off or filter through or get stuck in the brain, visual art seems to bypass our rational thoughts, defense mechanisms, prejudices, presumptions, and biases. Sometimes art gets to the heart of the matter, where a decision is made or a revelation is received.

Thanks to everyone who has helped NakedPastor cartoons spread across the world. Some say the cartoons have viral power, spreading far beyond my original audience. Others compare it to good news.

I guess it's the power of art.

—David Hayward, the artist behind @nakedpastor

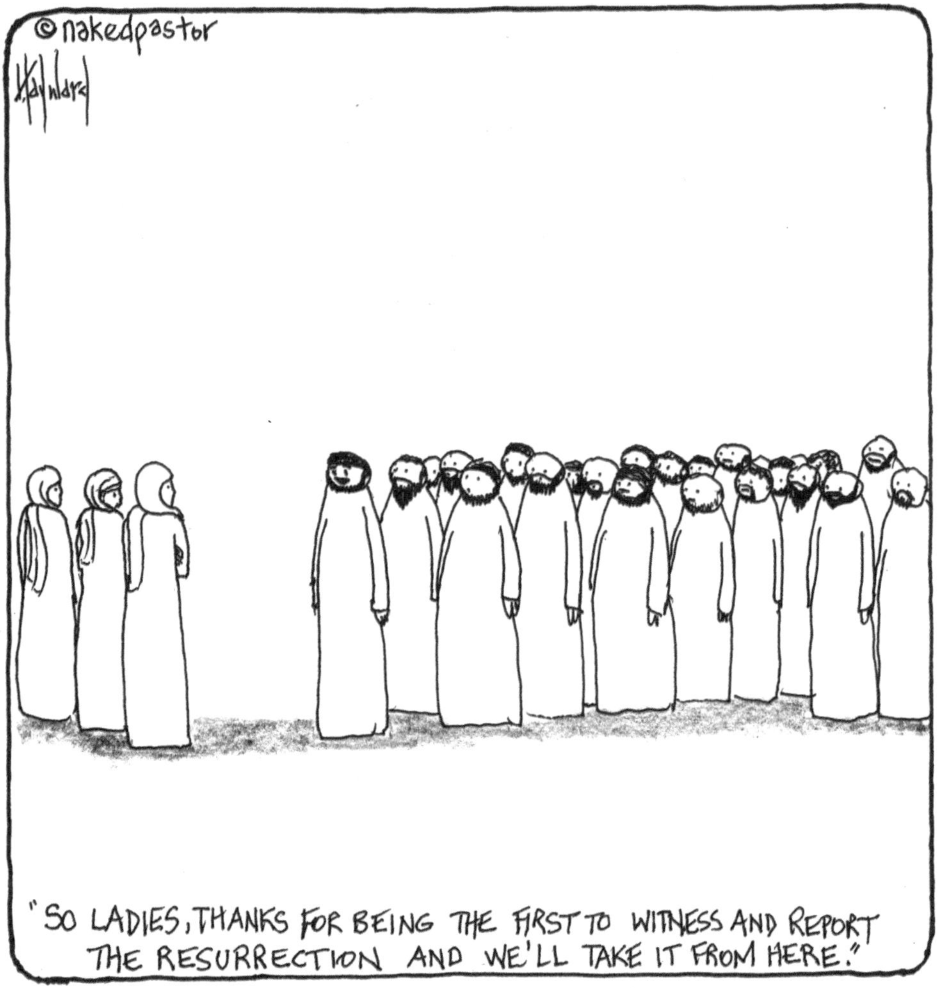
©nakedpastor

"SO LADIES, THANKS FOR BEING THE FIRST TO WITNESS AND REPORT THE RESURRECTION AND WE'LL TAKE IT FROM HERE."

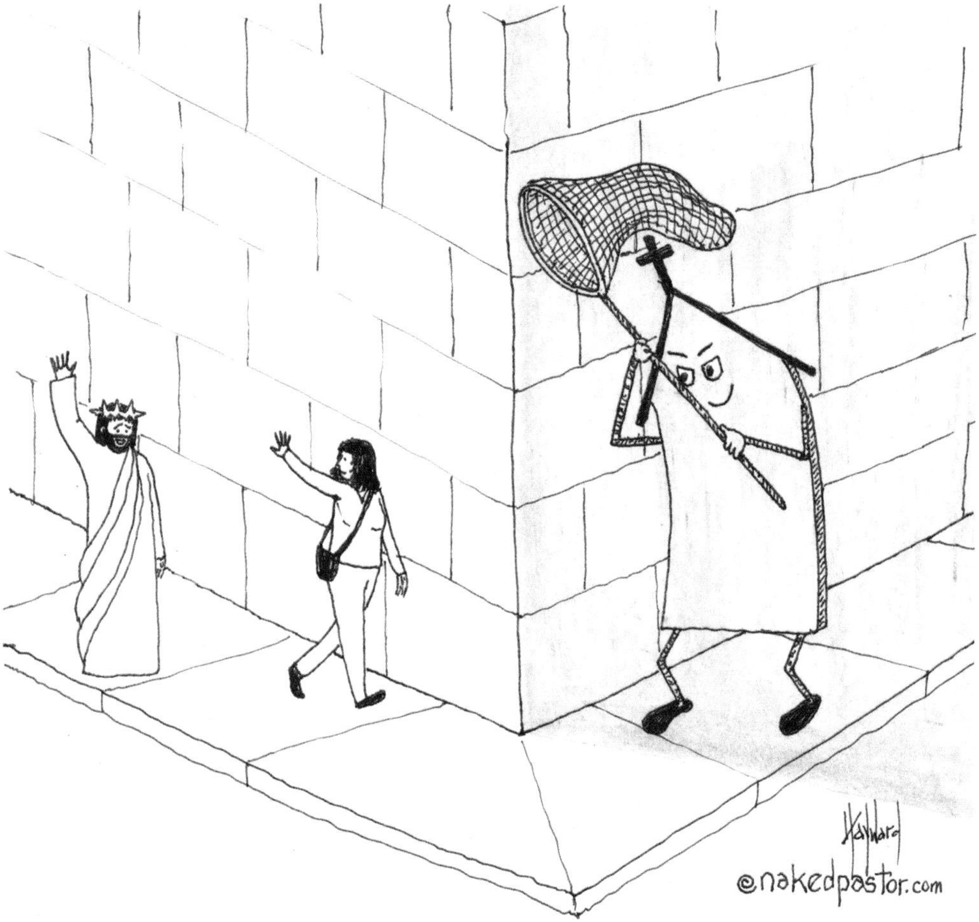
Hayward
©nakedpastor.com

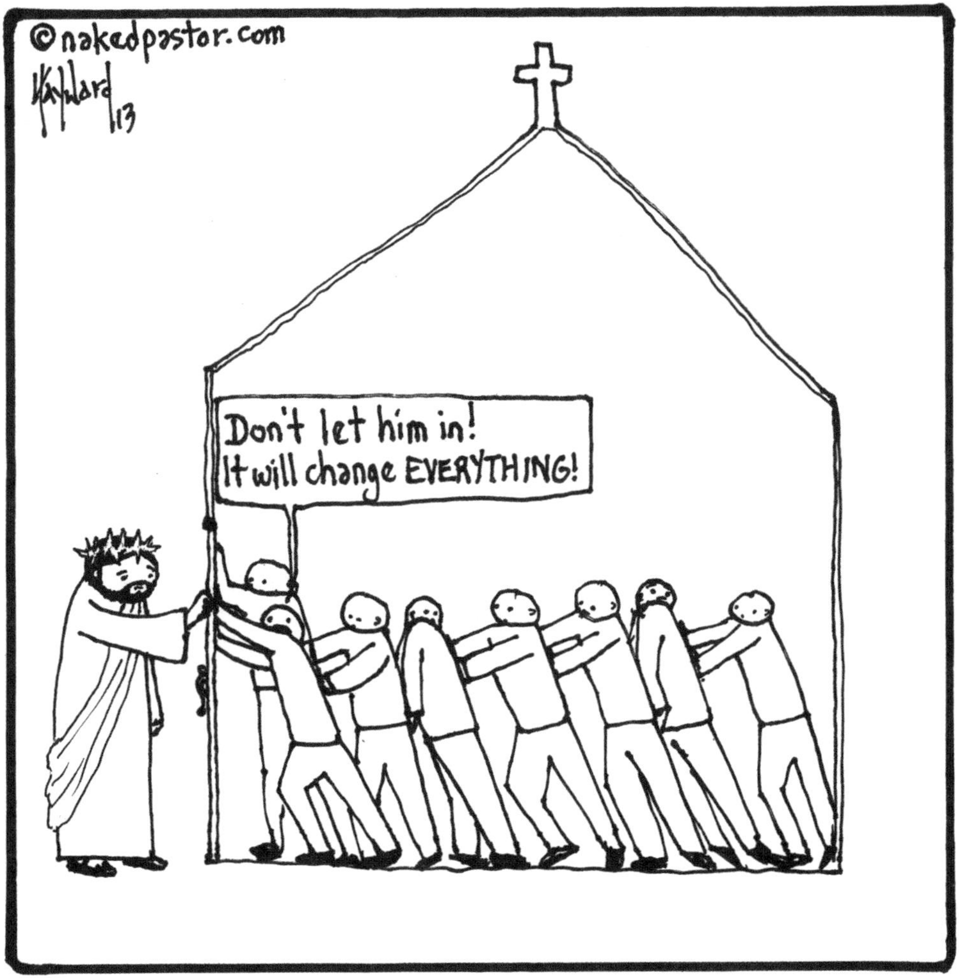
©nakedpastor.com
Don't let him in!
It will change EVERYTHING!

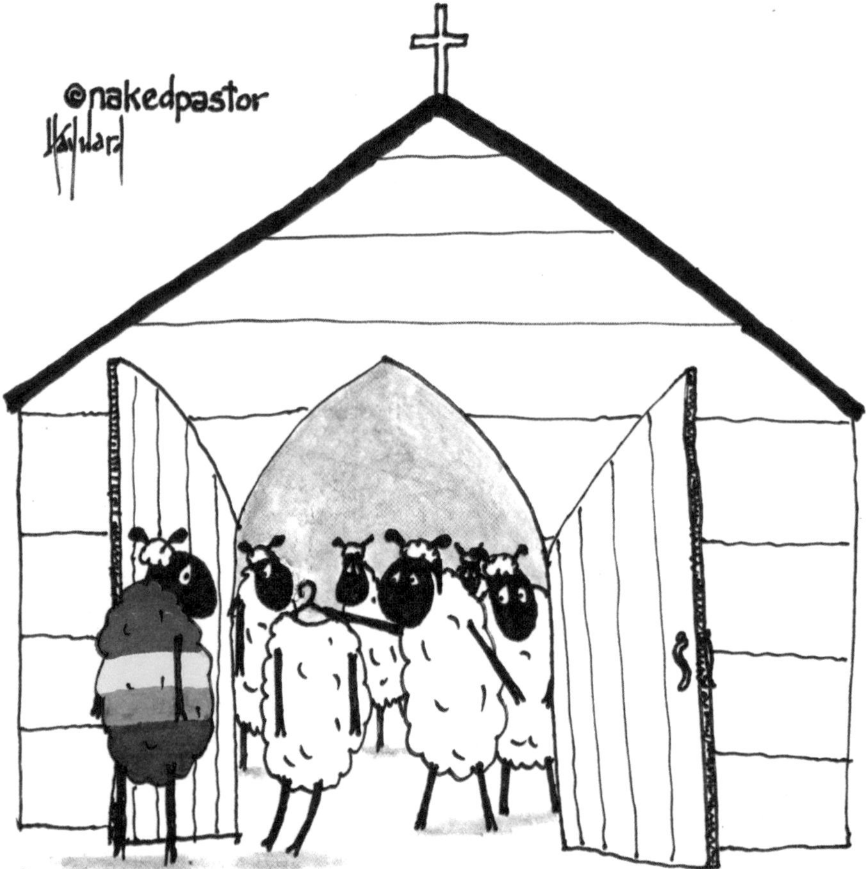
@nakedpastor
Hayward

"WELCOME! NOW JUST PUT THIS ON BEFORE COMING IN."

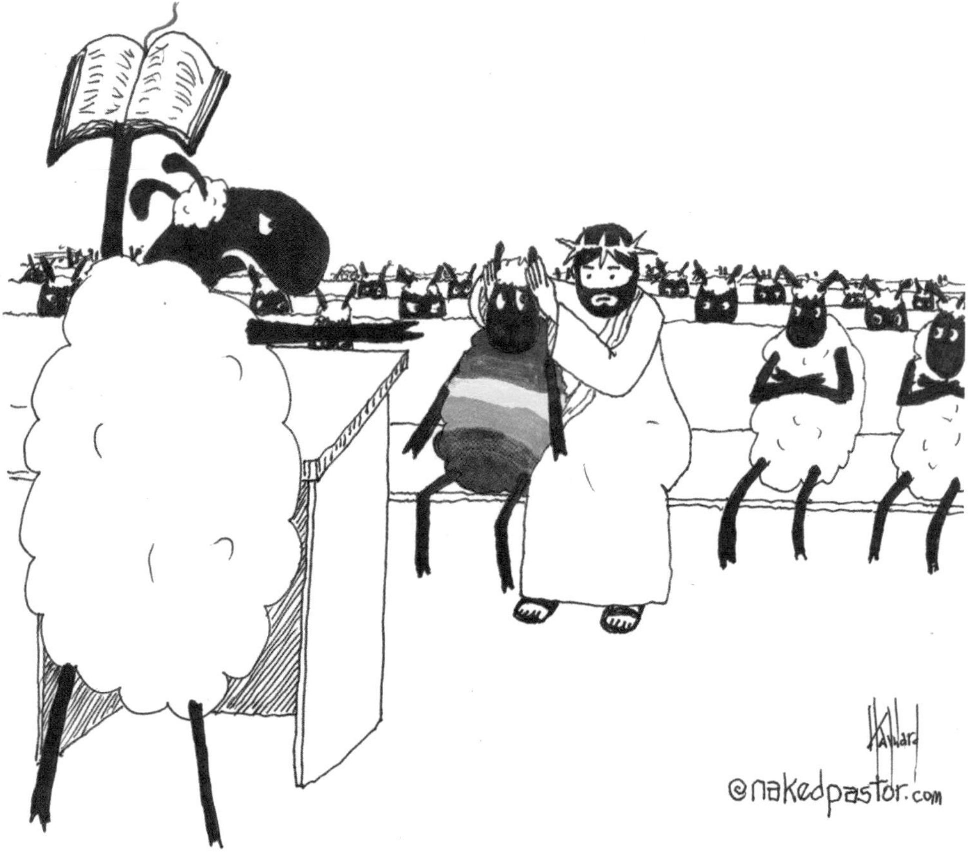
Hayward
©nakedpastor.com

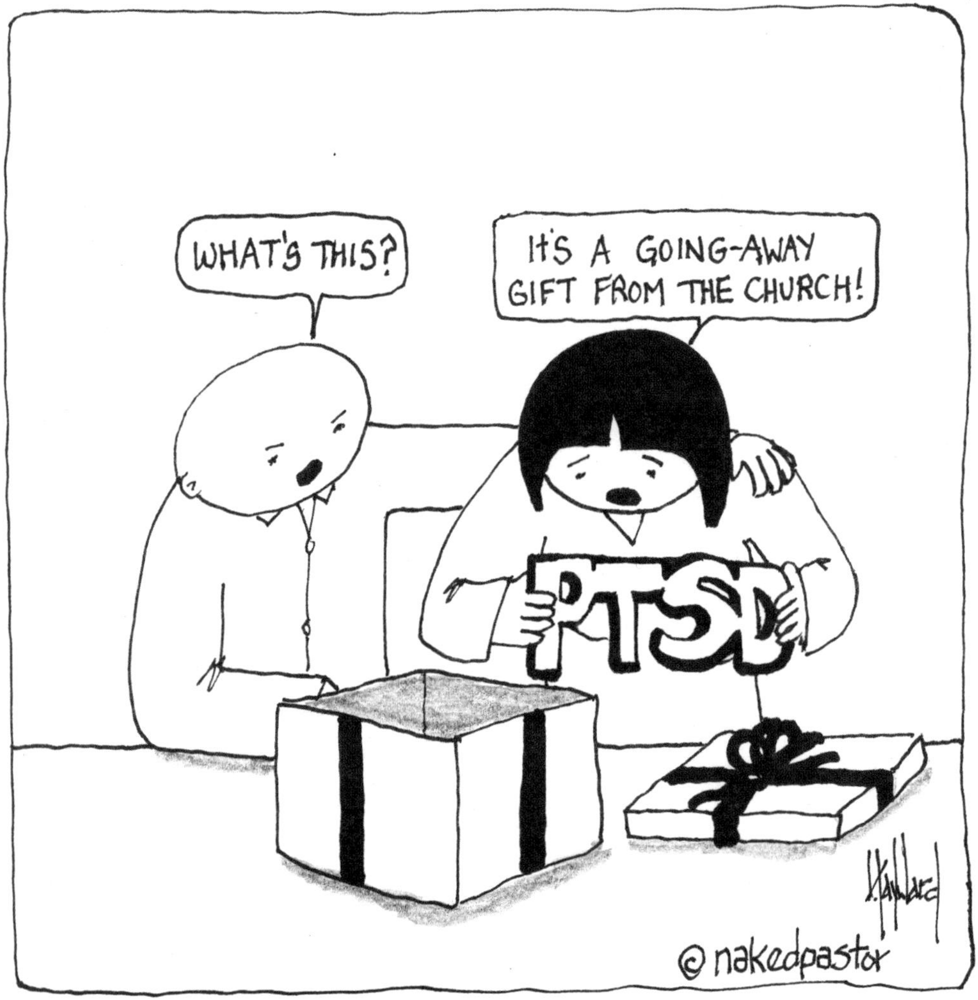
WHAT'S THIS?
IT'S A GOING-AWAY GIFT FROM THE CHURCH!
PTSD
© nakedpastor

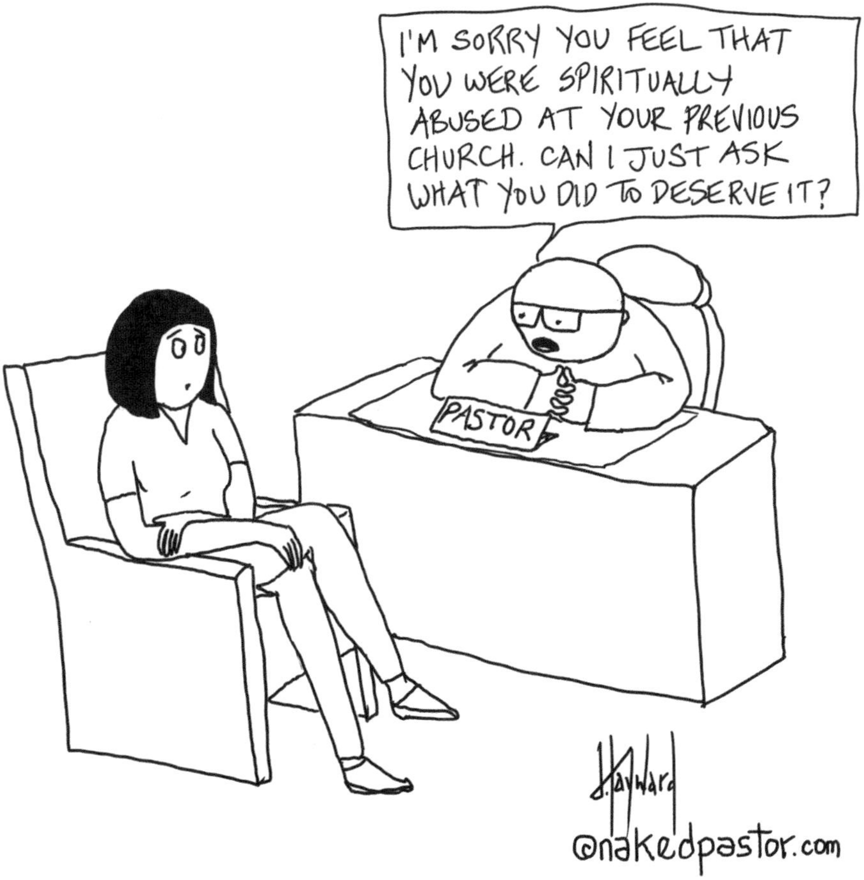
I'M SORRY YOU FEEL THAT YOU WERE SPIRITUALLY ABUSED AT YOUR PREVIOUS CHURCH. CAN I JUST ASK WHAT YOU DID TO DESERVE IT?
PASTOR
D. Hayward
©nakedpastor.com

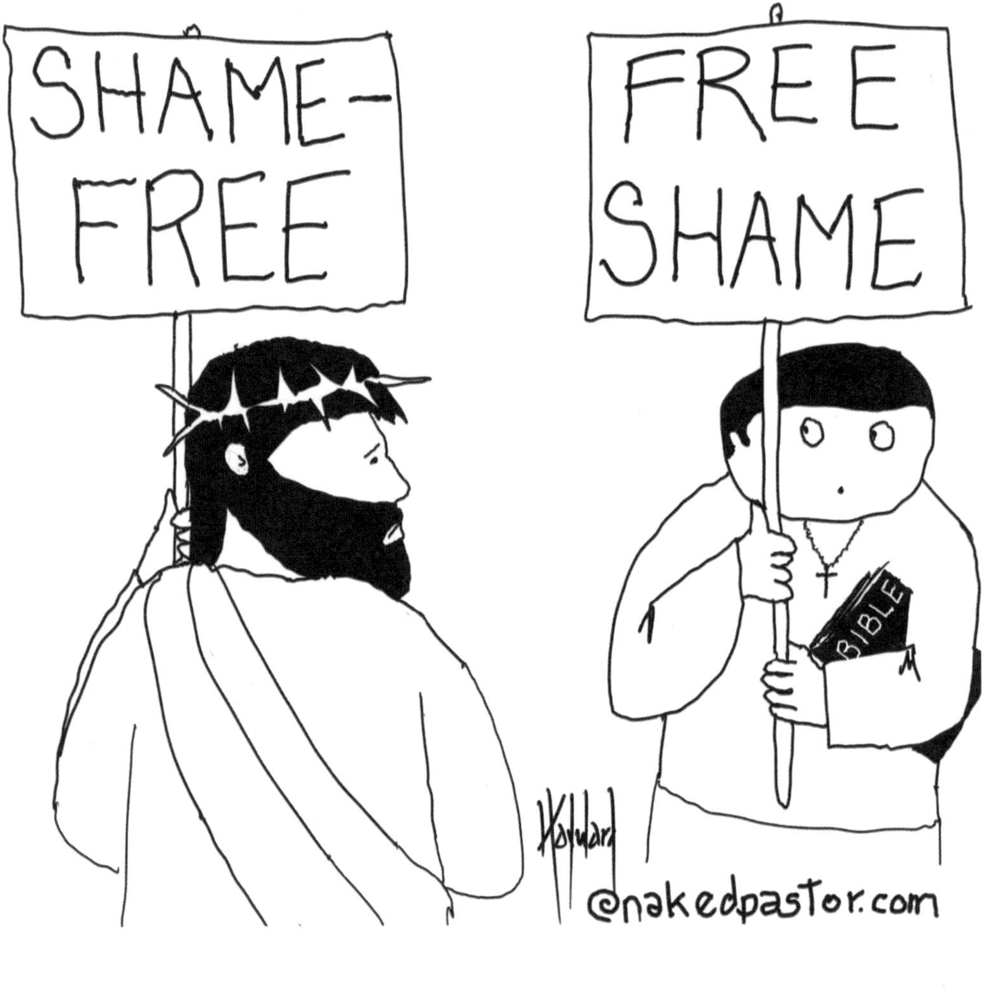
SHAME-FREE
FREE SHAME
BIBLE
@nakedpastor.com

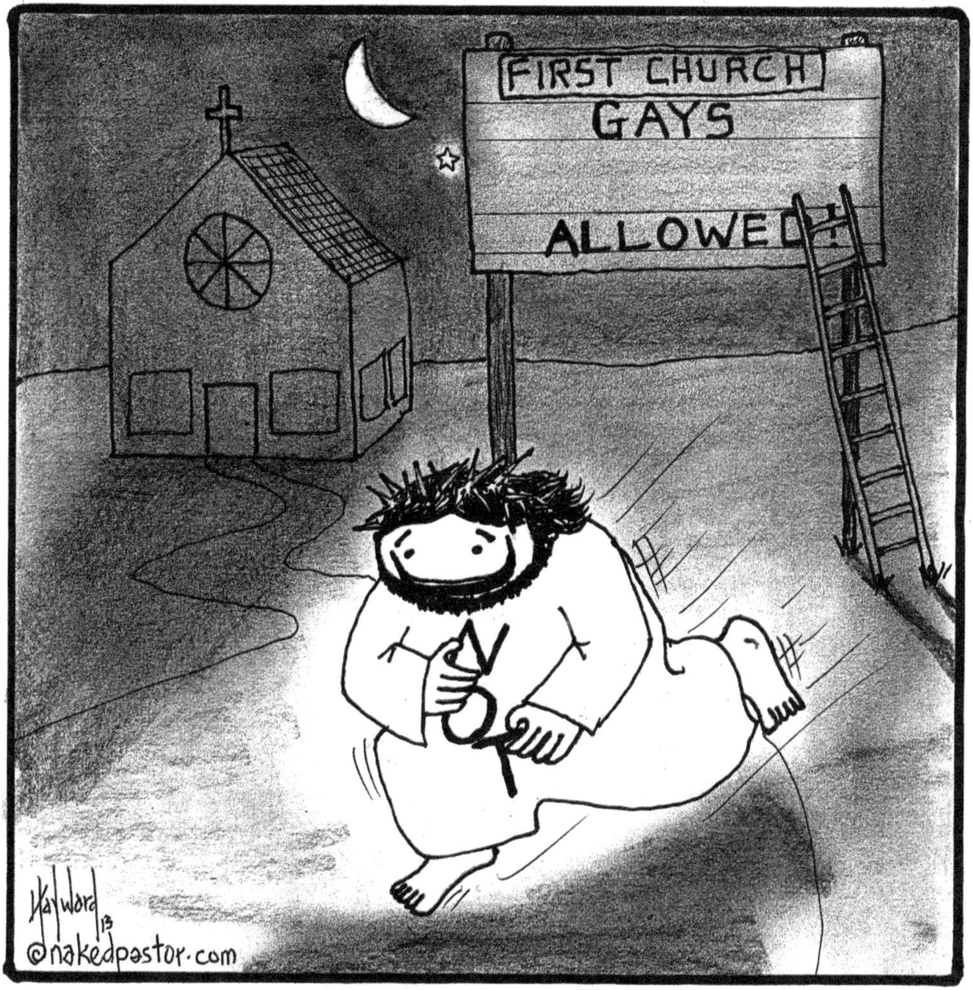
FIRST CHURCH
GAYS
ALLOWED!
NOT
Hayward 13
©nakedpastor.com

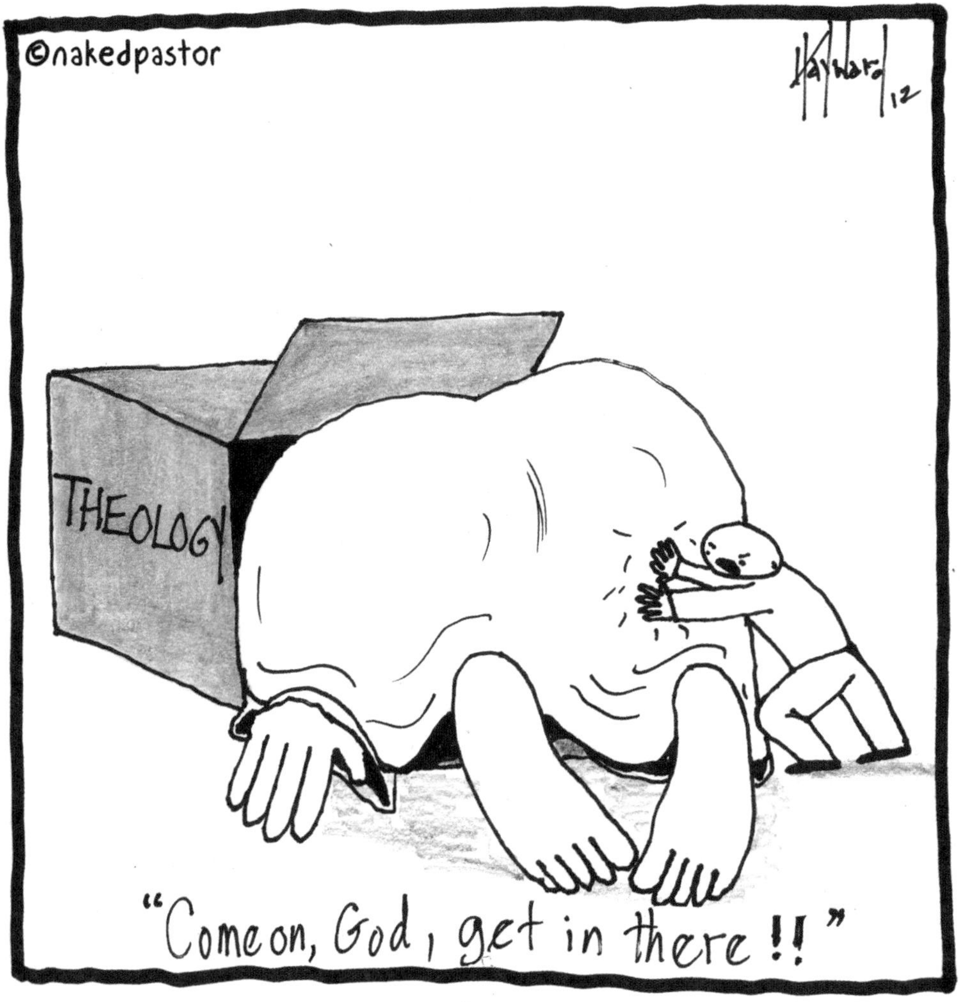
©nakedpastor
Hayward '12
THEOLOGY
"Come on, God, get in there!!"

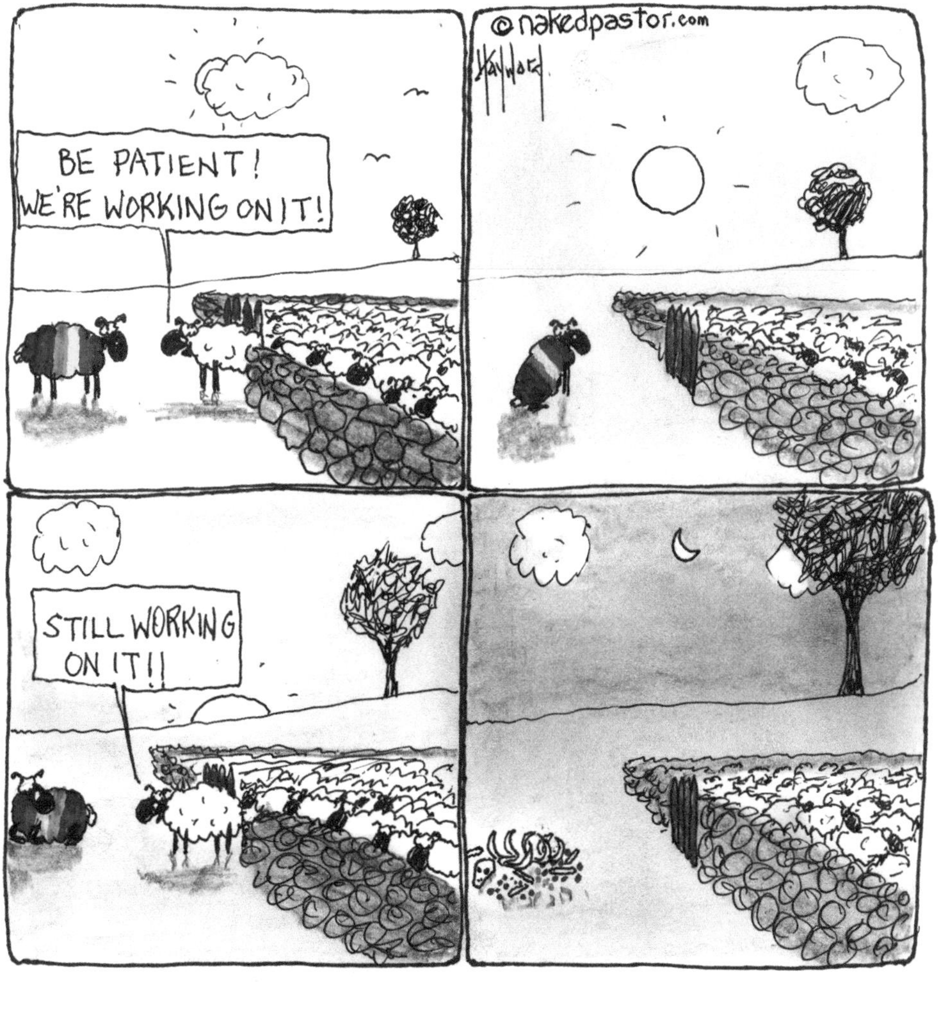
BE PATIENT! WE'RE WORKING ON IT!
©nakedpastor.com
Hayward
STILL WORKING ON IT!!

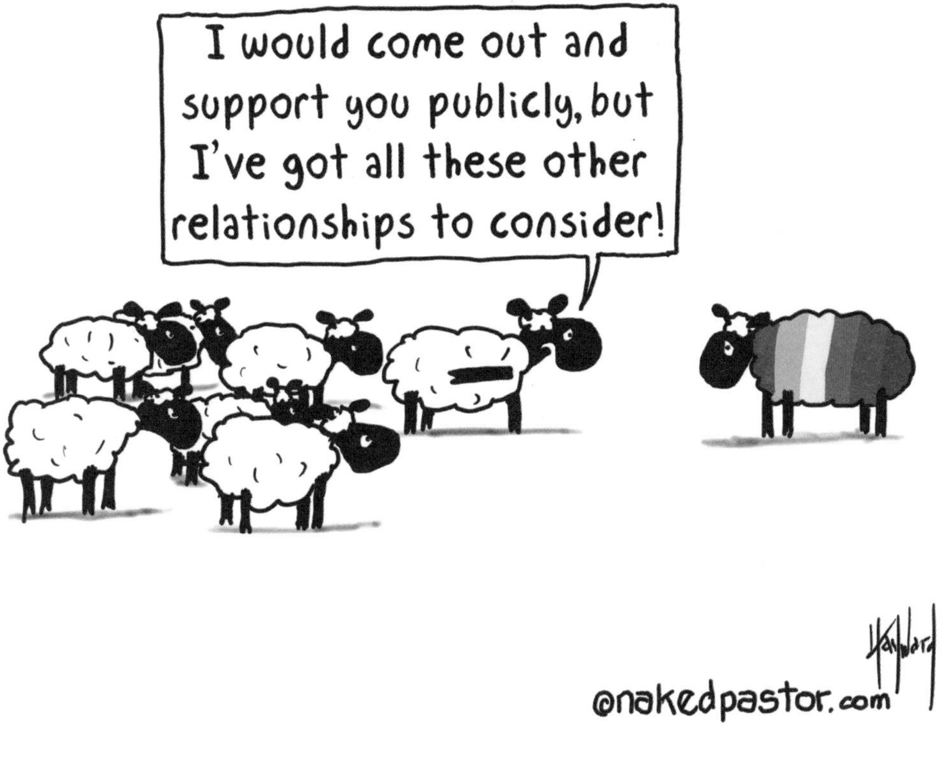
I would come out and support you publicly, but I've got all these other relationships to consider!
@nakedpastor.com

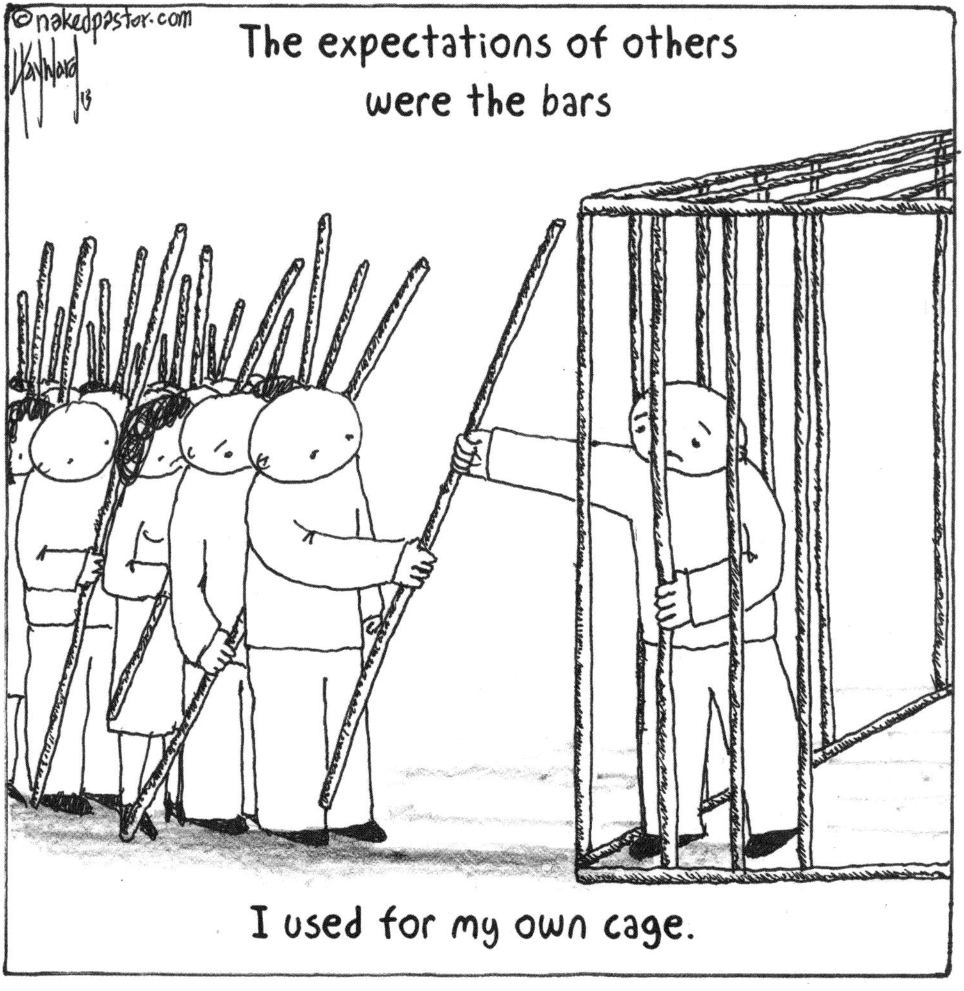
©nakedpastor.com
The expectations of others
were the bars
I used for my own cage.

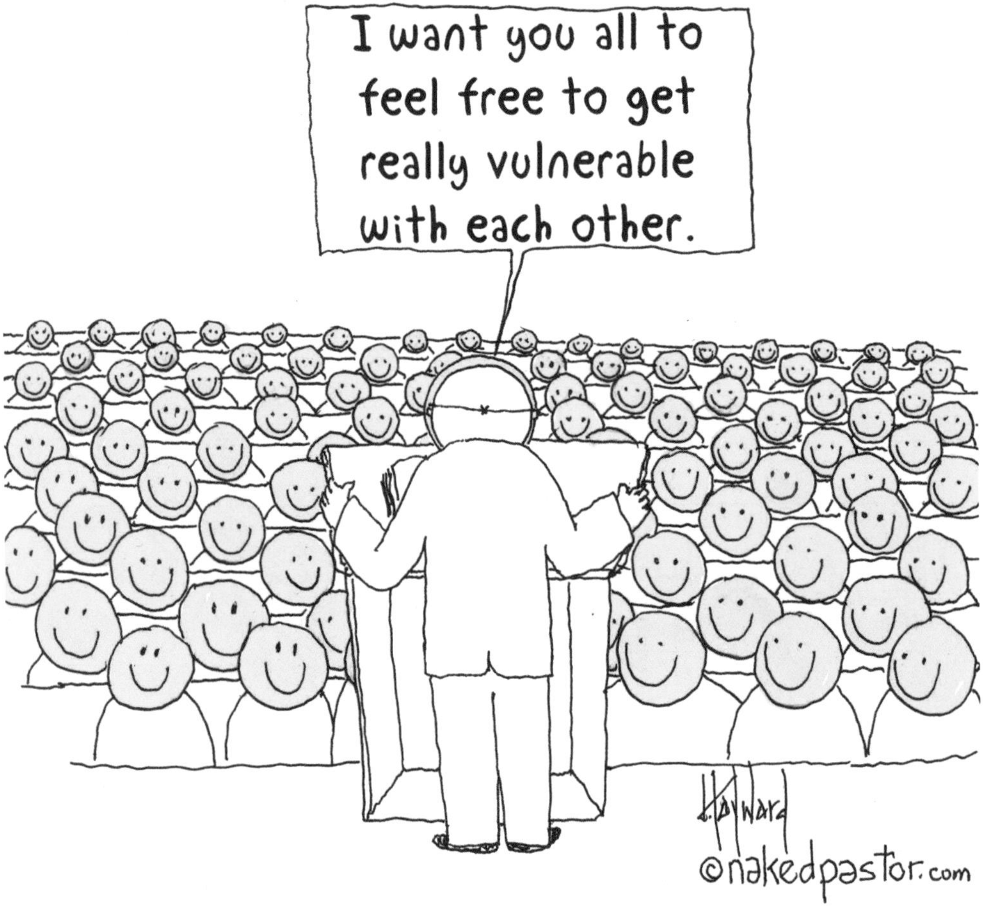
I want you all to feel free to get really vulnerable with each other.
Hayward
©nakedpastor.com

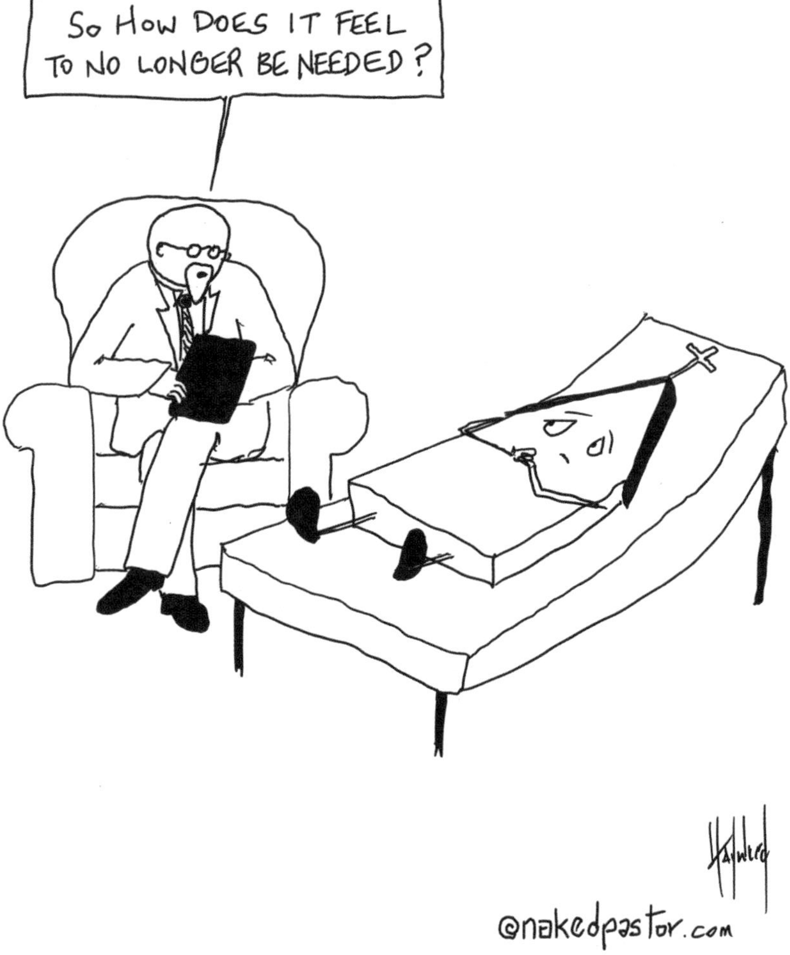
So HOW DOES IT FEEL TO NO LONGER BE NEEDED?
@nakedpastor.com

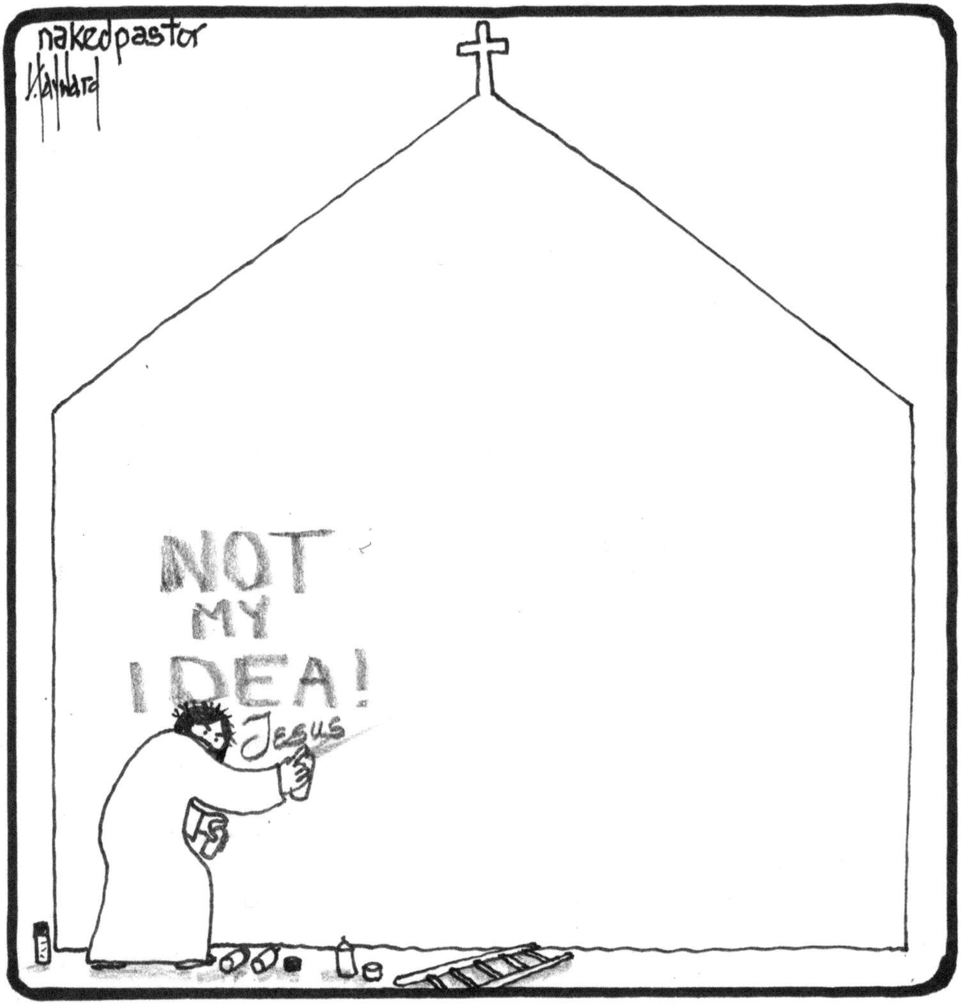
nakedpastor
Hayward
NOT
MY
IDEA!
Jesus

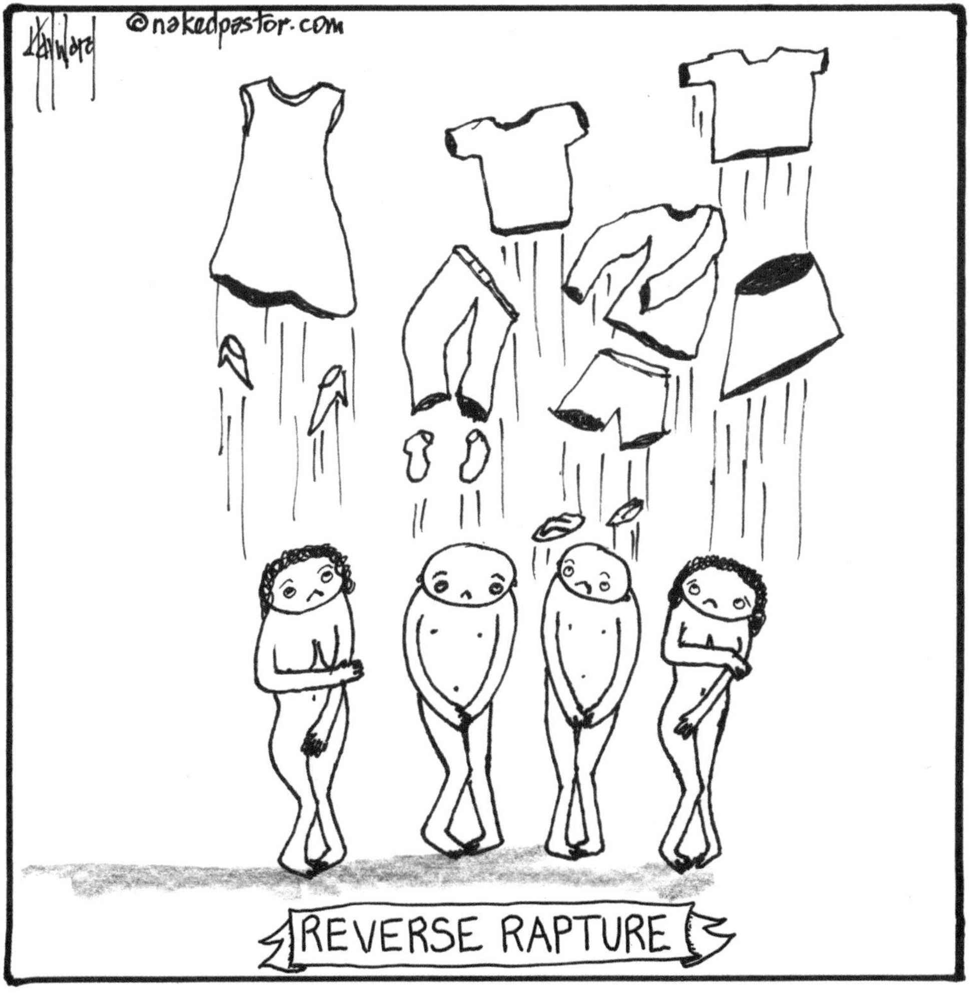
©nakedpastor.com
REVERSE RAPTURE

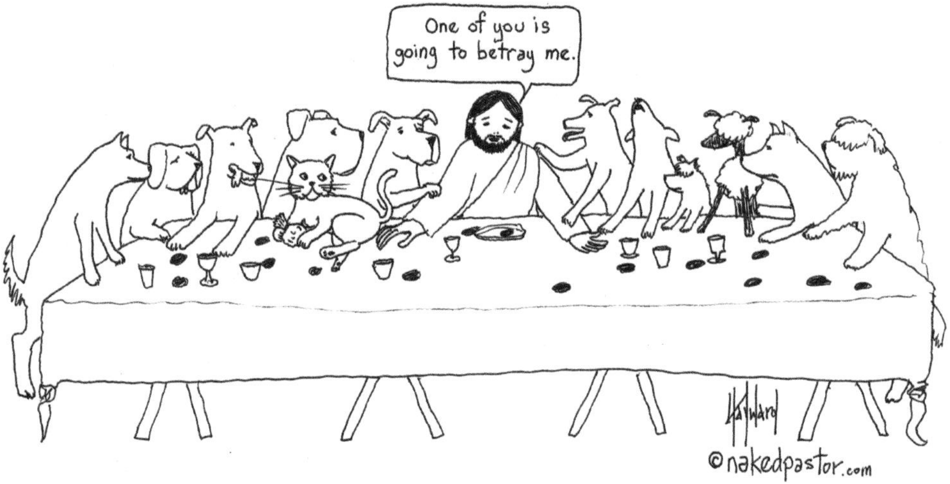
One of you is going to betray me.
Hayward
©nakedpastor.com

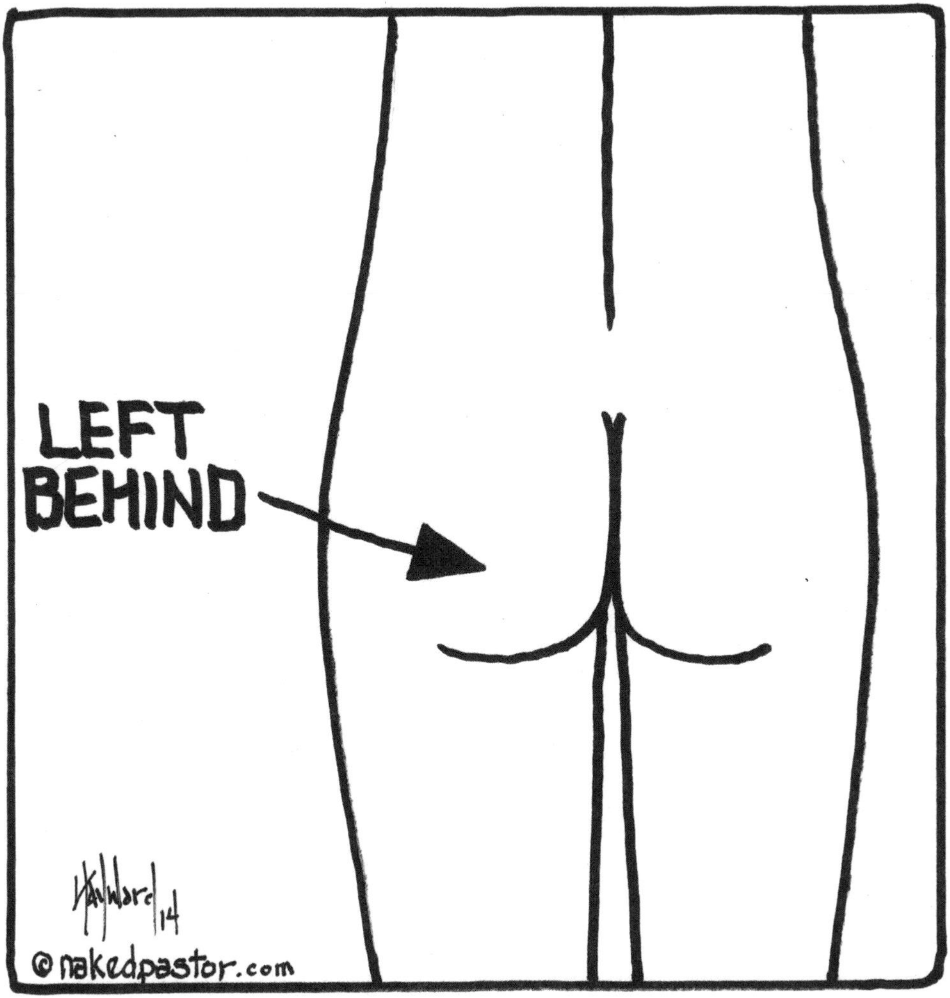
LEFT
BEHIND
©nakedpastor.com

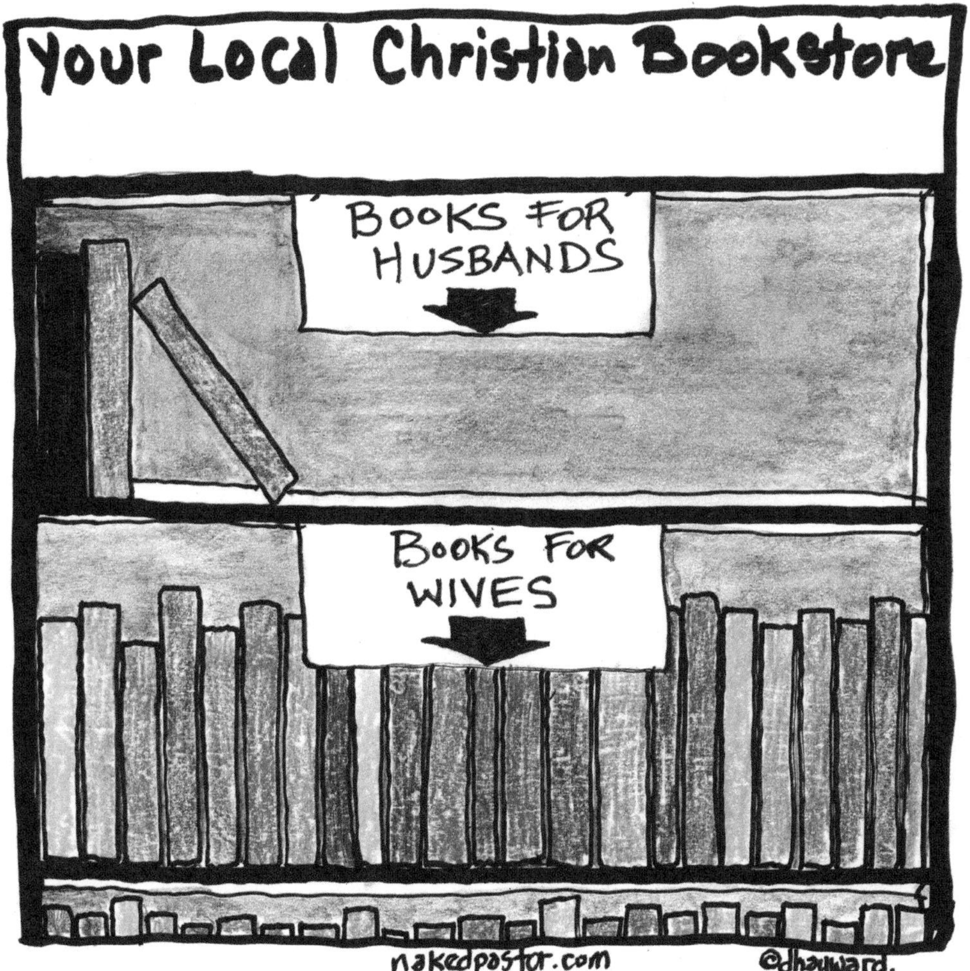
Your Local Christian Bookstore
BOOKS FOR HUSBANDS
BOOKS FOR WIVES
nakedpastor.com
@dhayward.

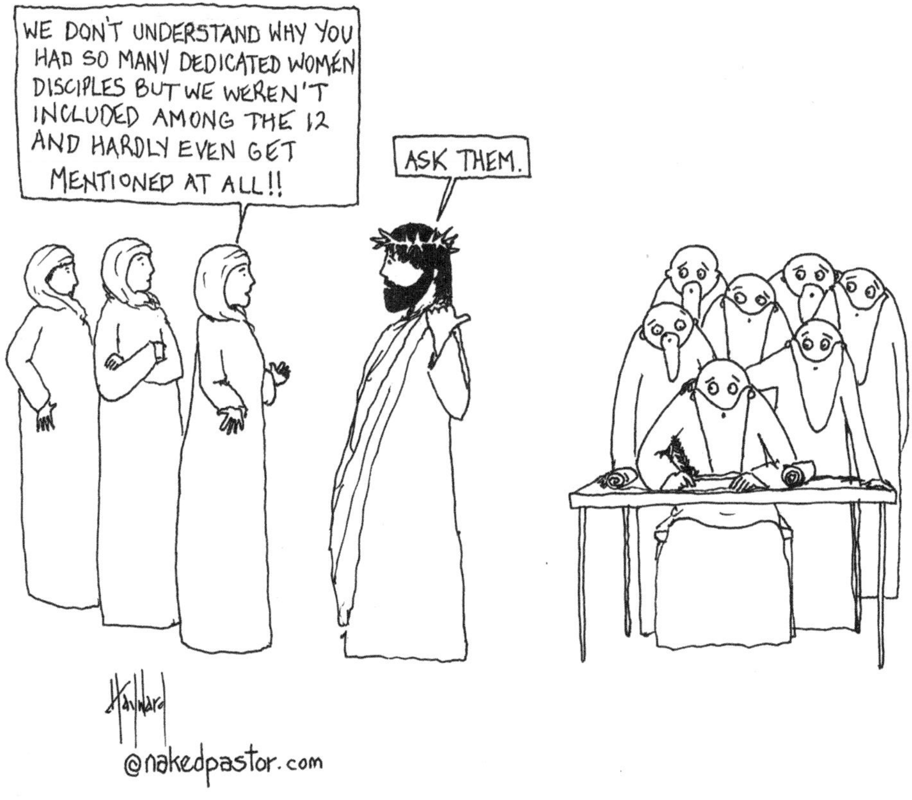
WE DON'T UNDERSTAND WHY YOU HAD SO MANY DEDICATED WOMEN DISCIPLES BUT WE WEREN'T INCLUDED AMONG THE 12 AND HARDLY EVEN GET MENTIONED AT ALL!!
ASK THEM.
Hayward
@nakedpastor.com

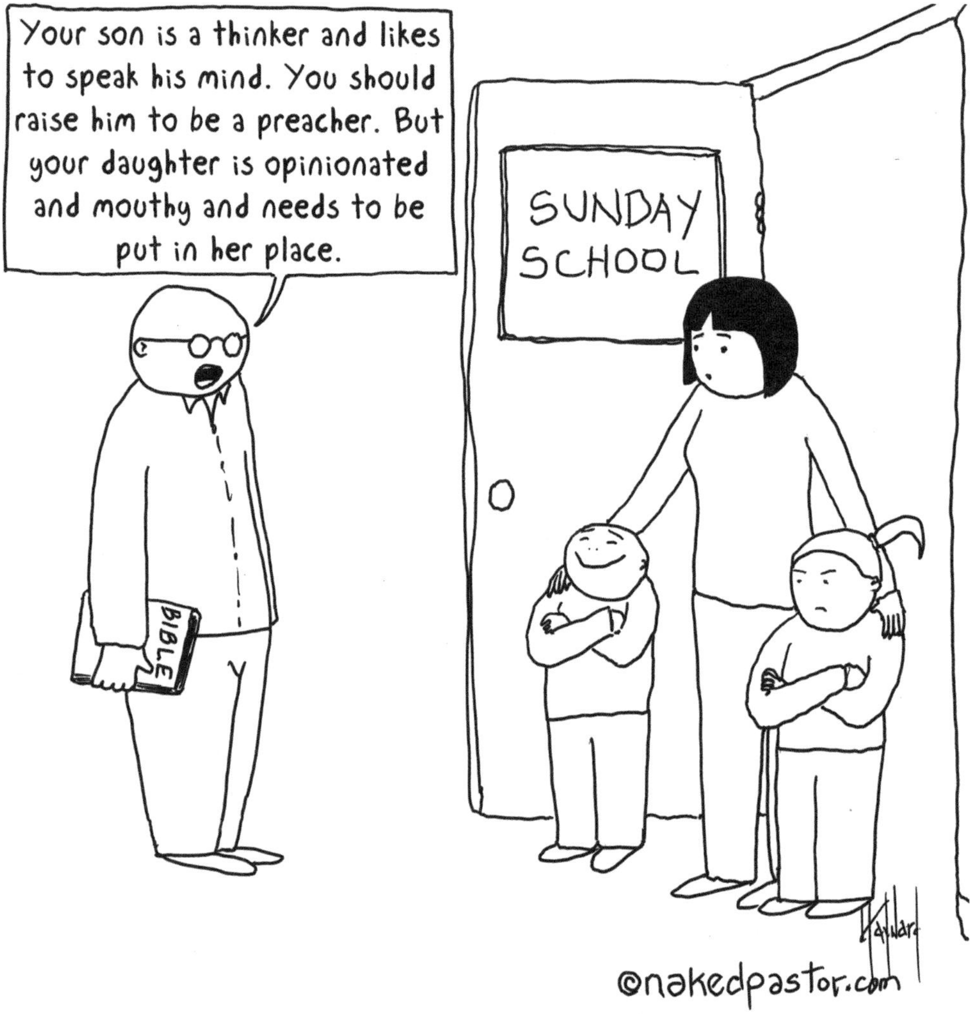
Your son is a thinker and likes to speak his mind. You should raise him to be a preacher. But your daughter is opinionated and mouthy and needs to be put in her place.
SUNDAY SCHOOL
BIBLE
Hayward
©nakedpastor.com

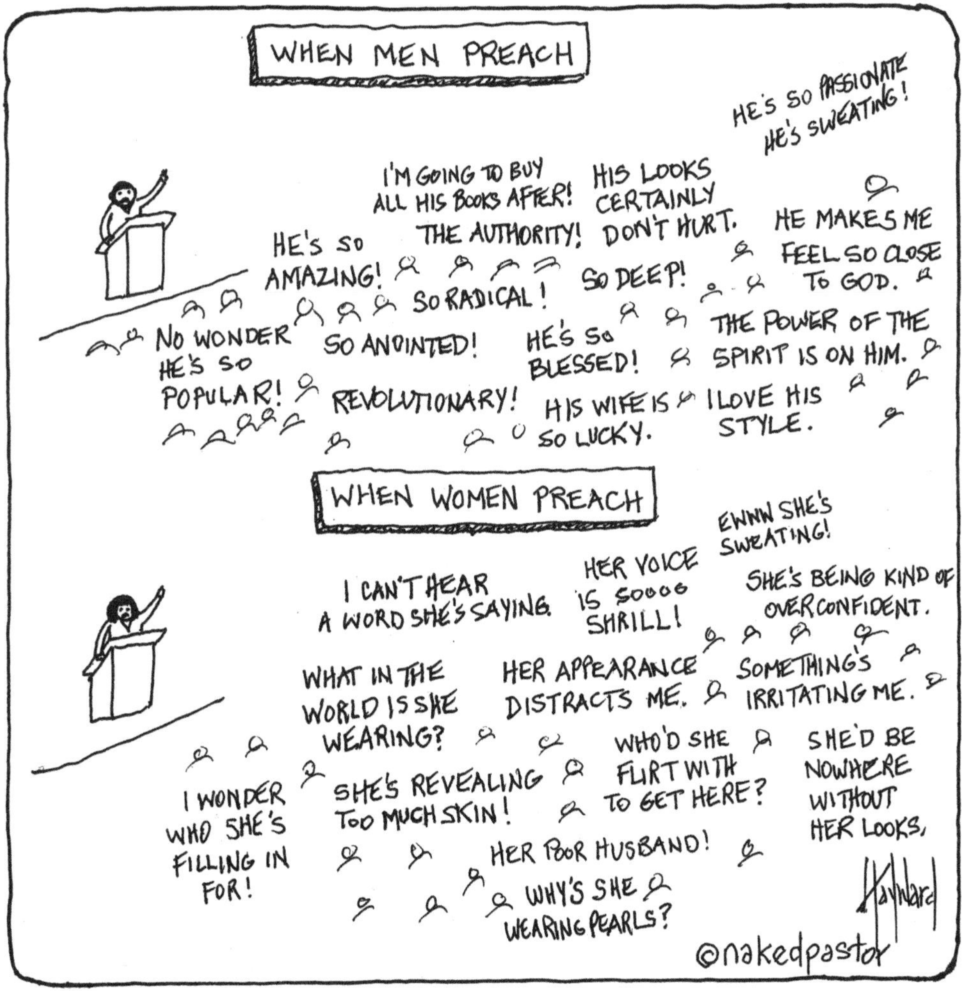
WHEN MEN PREACH
HE'S SO PASSIONATE HE'S SWEATING!
I'M GOING TO BUY ALL HIS BOOKS AFTER!
HIS LOOKS CERTAINLY DON'T HURT.
HE'S SO AMAZING!
THE AUTHORITY!
HE MAKES ME FEEL SO CLOSE TO GOD.
SO DEEP!
SO RADICAL!
NO WONDER HE'S SO POPULAR!
SO ANOINTED!
HE'S SO BLESSED!
THE POWER OF THE SPIRIT IS ON HIM.
REVOLUTIONARY!
HIS WIFE IS SO LUCKY.
I LOVE HIS STYLE.
WHEN WOMEN PREACH
EWWW SHE'S SWEATING!
I CAN'T HEAR A WORD SHE'S SAYING.
HER VOICE IS SOOOO SHRILL!
SHE'S BEING KIND OF OVERCONFIDENT.
WHAT IN THE WORLD IS SHE WEARING?
HER APPEARANCE DISTRACTS ME.
SOMETHING'S IRRITATING ME.
I WONDER WHO SHE'S FILLING IN FOR!
SHE'S REVEALING TOO MUCH SKIN!
WHO'D SHE FLIRT WITH TO GET HERE?
SHE'D BE NOWHERE WITHOUT HER LOOKS.
HER POOR HUSBAND!
WHY'S SHE WEARING PEARLS?
Hayward
©nakedpastor

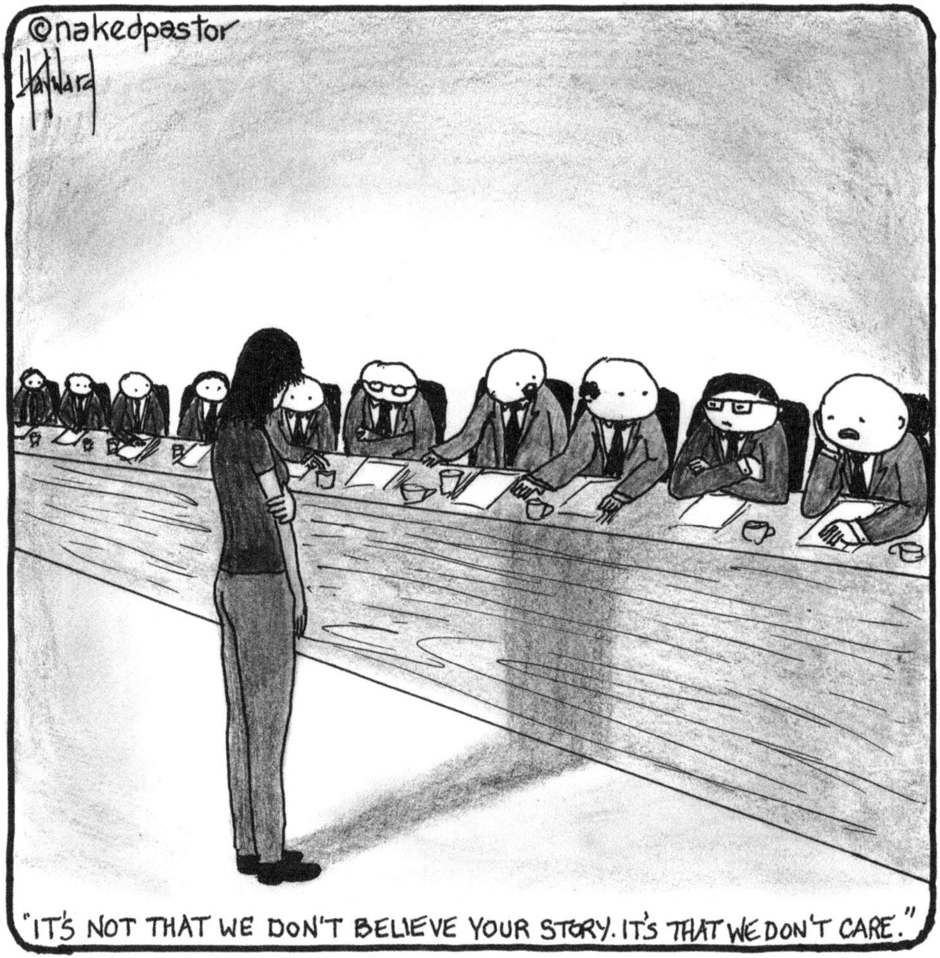
©nakedpastor
Hayward
"IT'S NOT THAT WE DON'T BELIEVE YOUR STORY. IT'S THAT WE DON'T CARE."

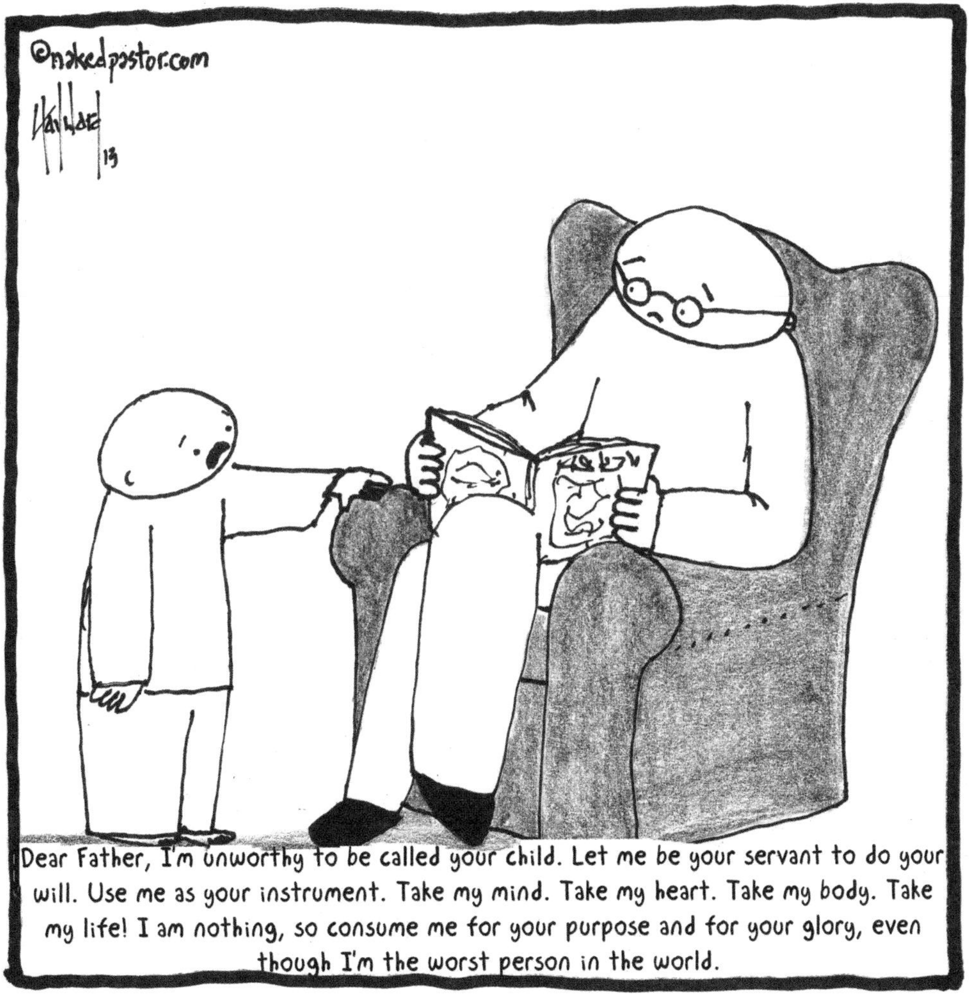
©nakedpastor.com
Dear Father, I'm unworthy to be called your child. Let me be your servant to do your will. Use me as your instrument. Take my mind. Take my heart. Take my body. Take my life! I am nothing, so consume me for your purpose and for your glory, even though I'm the worst person in the world.

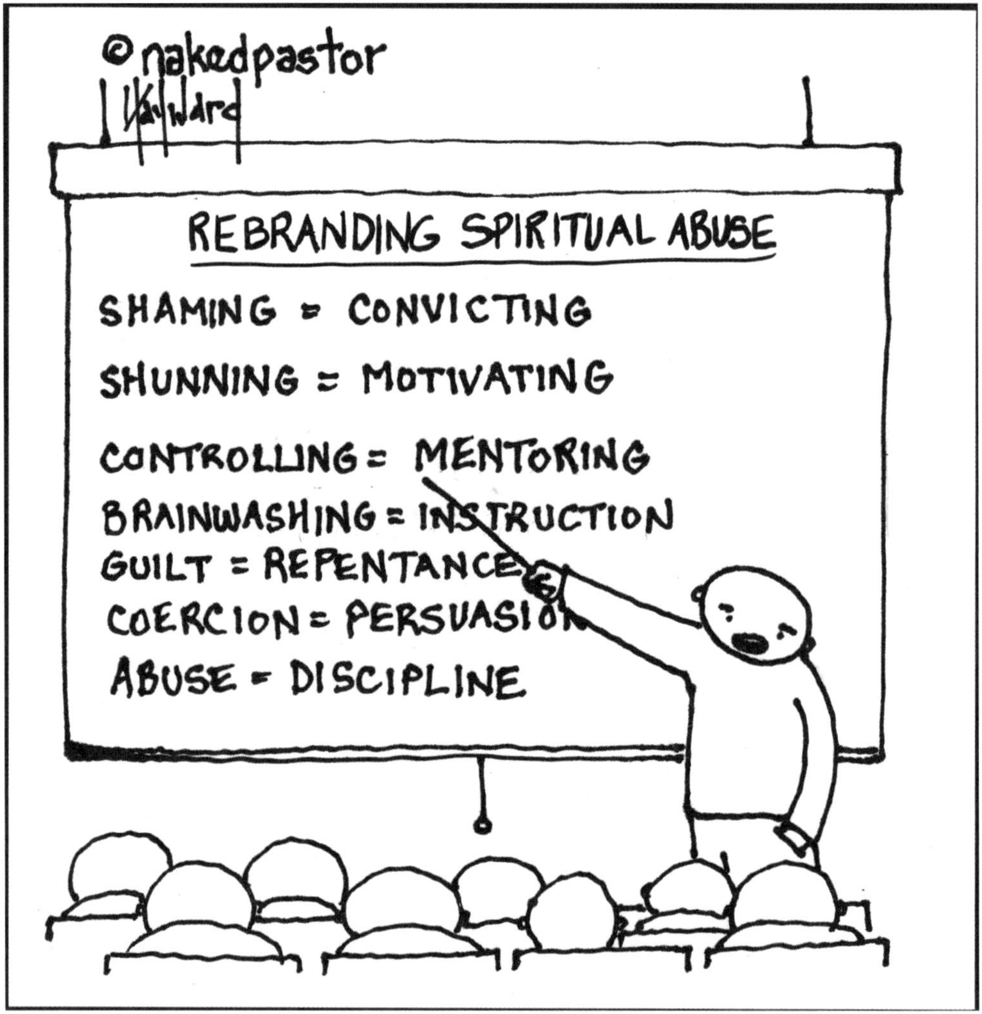

© nakedpastor
Hayward
REBRANDING SPIRITUAL ABUSE
SHAMING = CONVICTING
SHUNNING = MOTIVATING
CONTROLLING = MENTORING
BRAINWASHING = INSTRUCTION
GUILT = REPENTANCE
COERCION = PERSUASION
ABUSE = DISCIPLINE

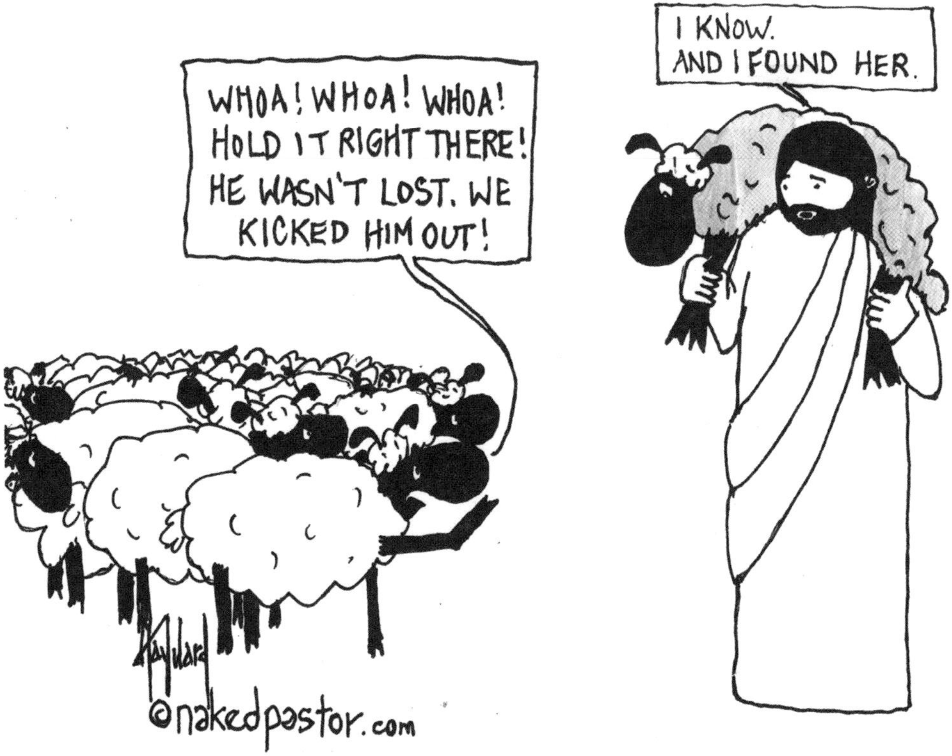
WHOA! WHOA! WHOA! HOLD IT RIGHT THERE! HE WASN'T LOST. WE KICKED HIM OUT!
I KNOW. AND I FOUND HER.
©nakedpastor.com

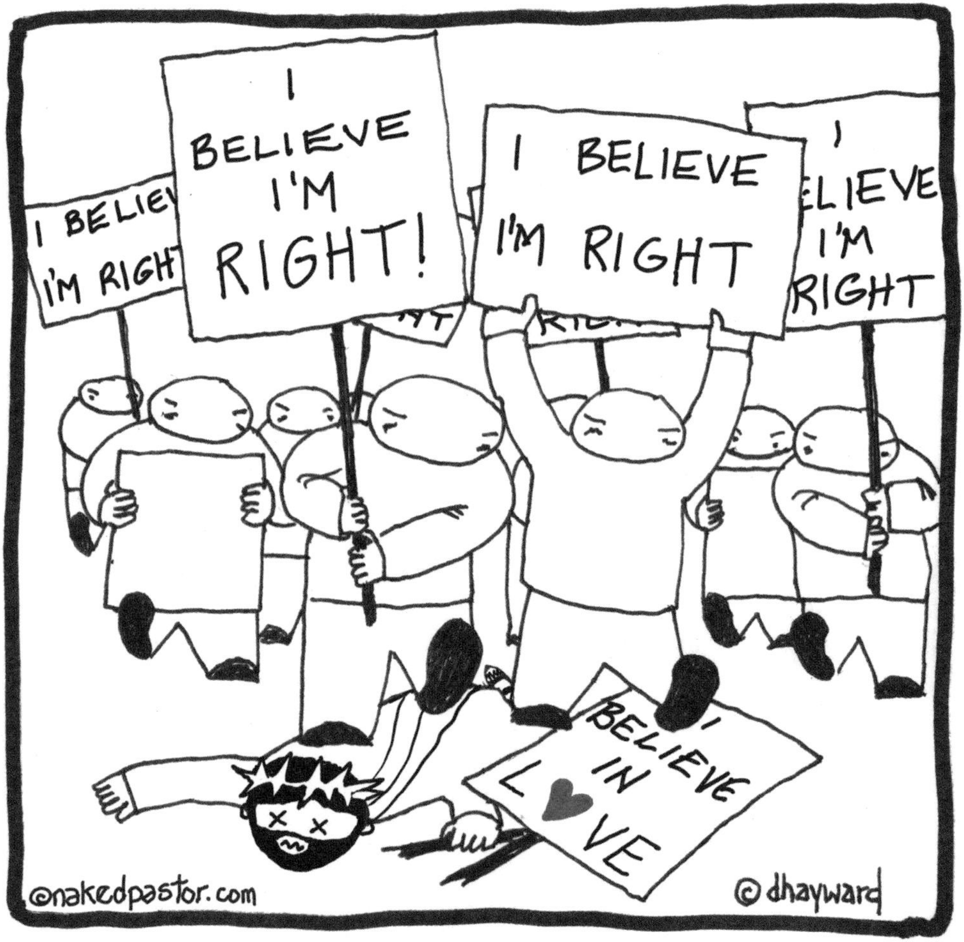
I BELIEV
I'M RIGH
I BELIEVE I'M RIGHT!
I BELIEVE I'M RIGHT
ELIEVE I'M RIGHT
I BELIEVE IN L♥VE
©nakedpastor.com
© dhayward

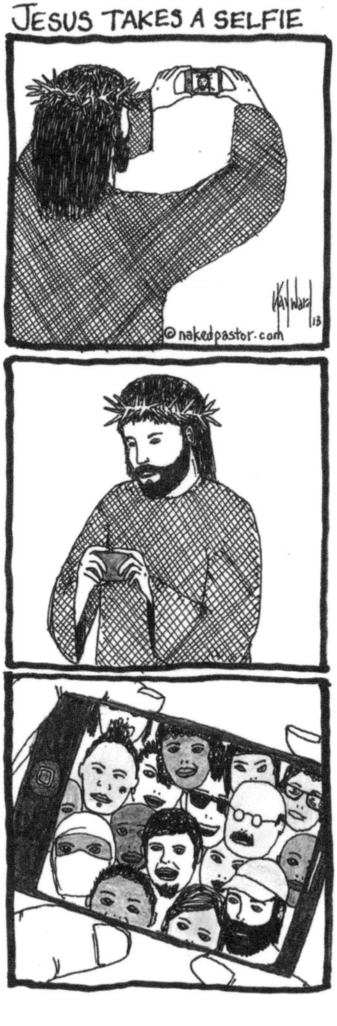
JESUS TAKES A SELFIE
©nakedpastor.com

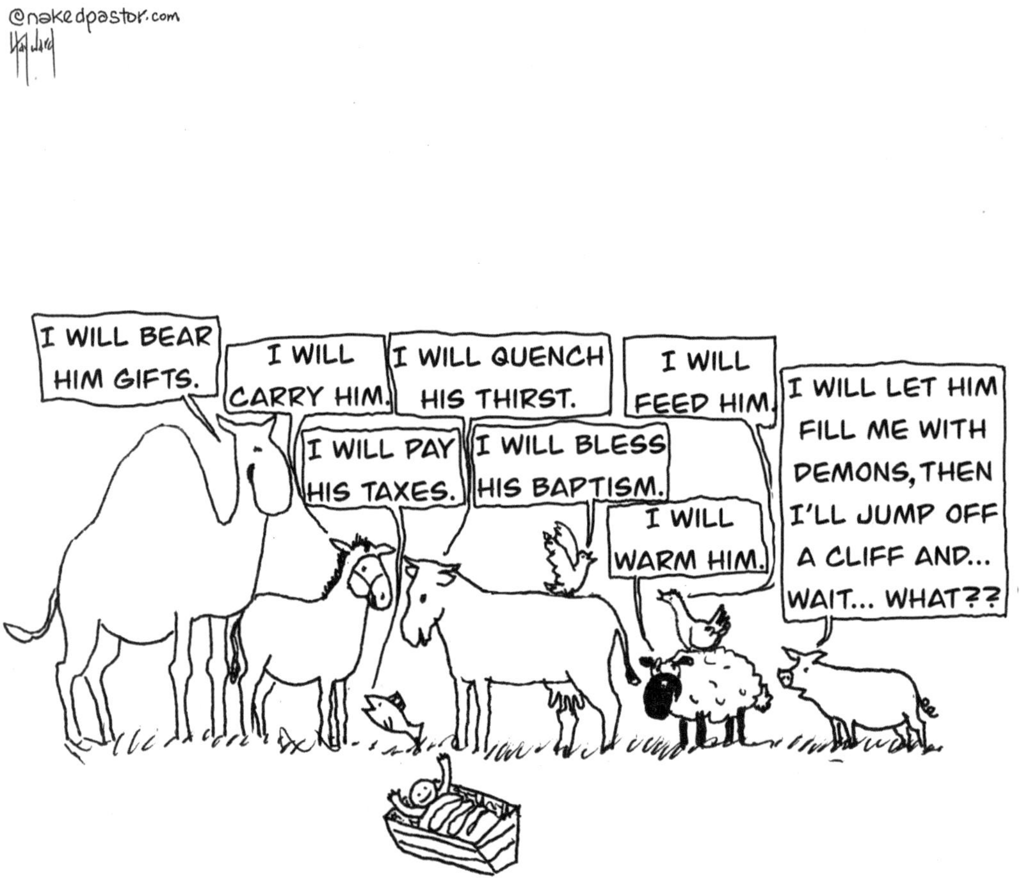
@nakedpastor.com
I WILL BEAR HIM GIFTS.
I WILL CARRY HIM.
I WILL QUENCH HIS THIRST.
I WILL FEED HIM.
I WILL LET HIM FILL ME WITH DEMONS, THEN I'LL JUMP OFF A CLIFF AND... WAIT... WHAT??
I WILL PAY HIS TAXES.
I WILL BLESS HIS BAPTISM.
I WILL WARM HIM.

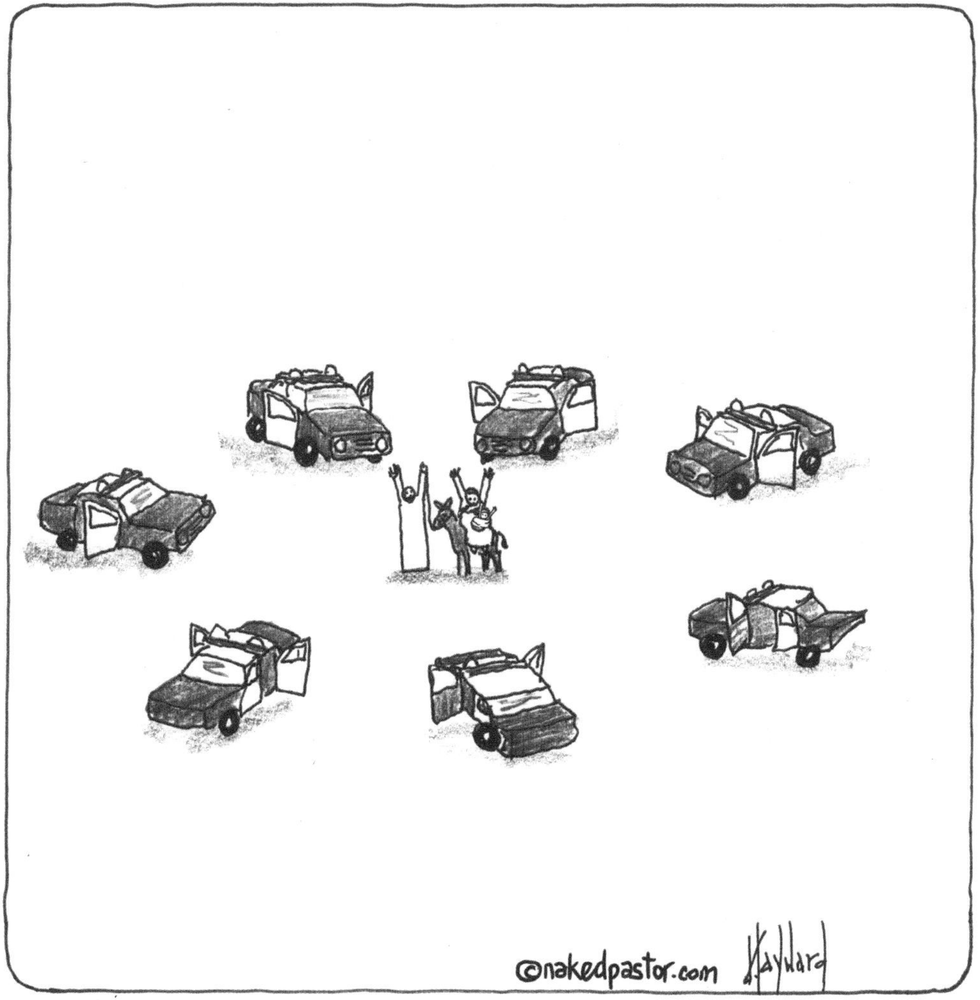
©nakedpastor.com
Hayward

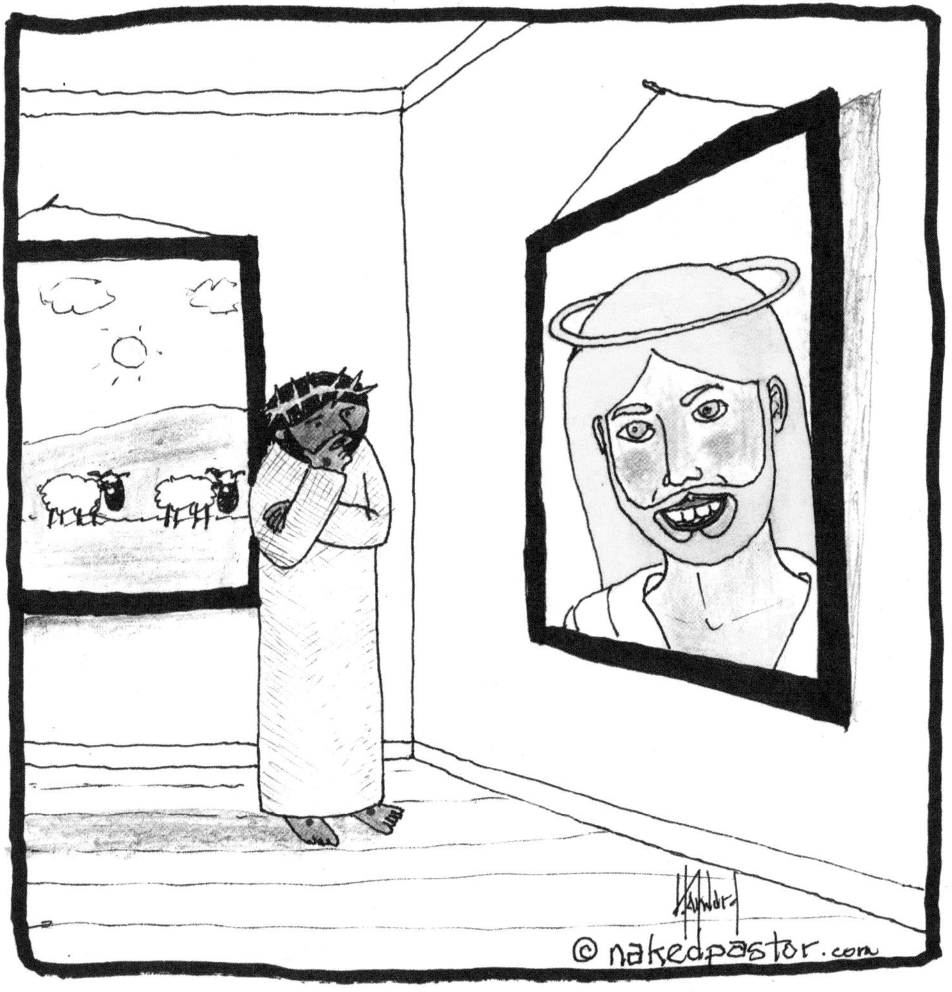
© nakedpastor.com

TWO VIEWS
GOD
GOD
@nakedpastor

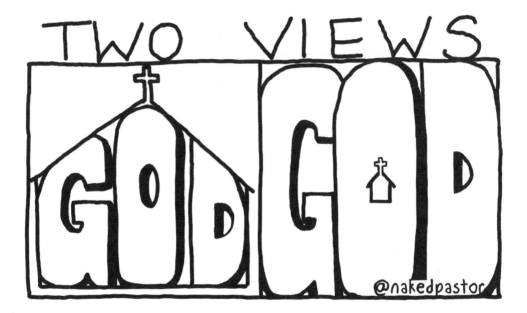

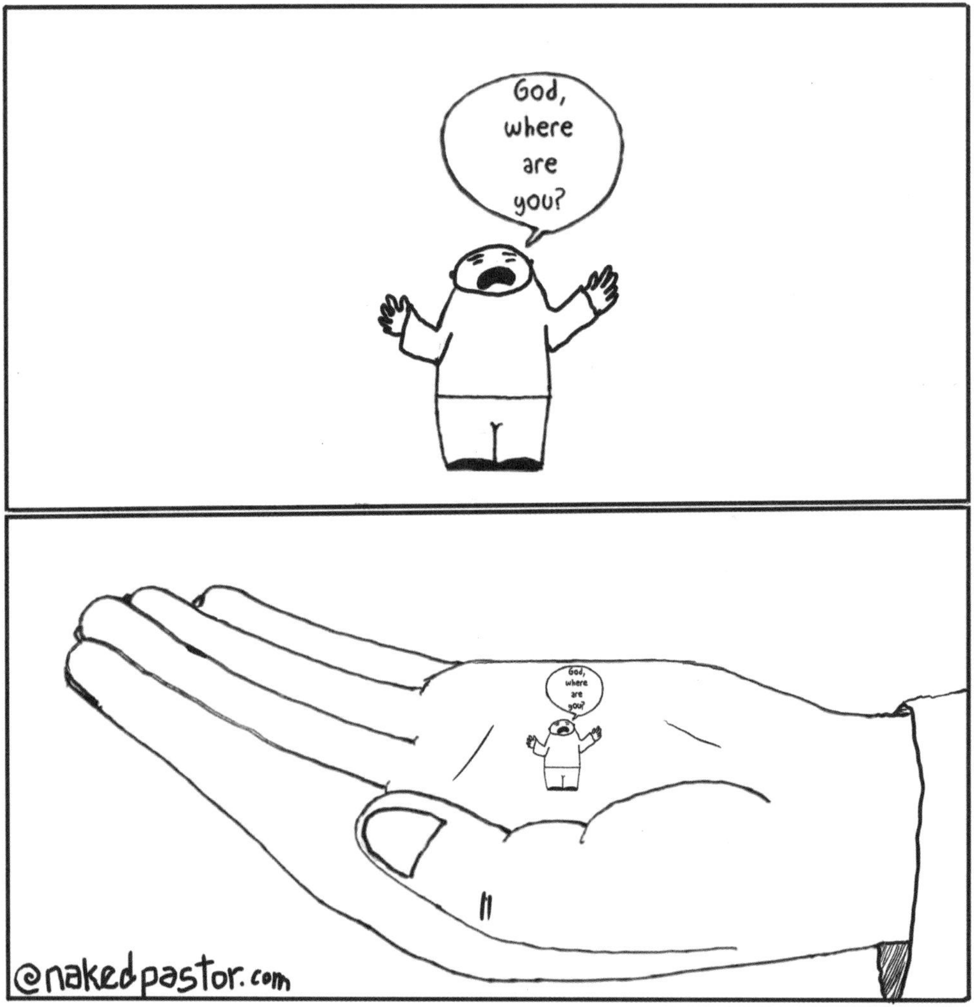
God, where are you?
God, where are you?
@nakedpastor.com

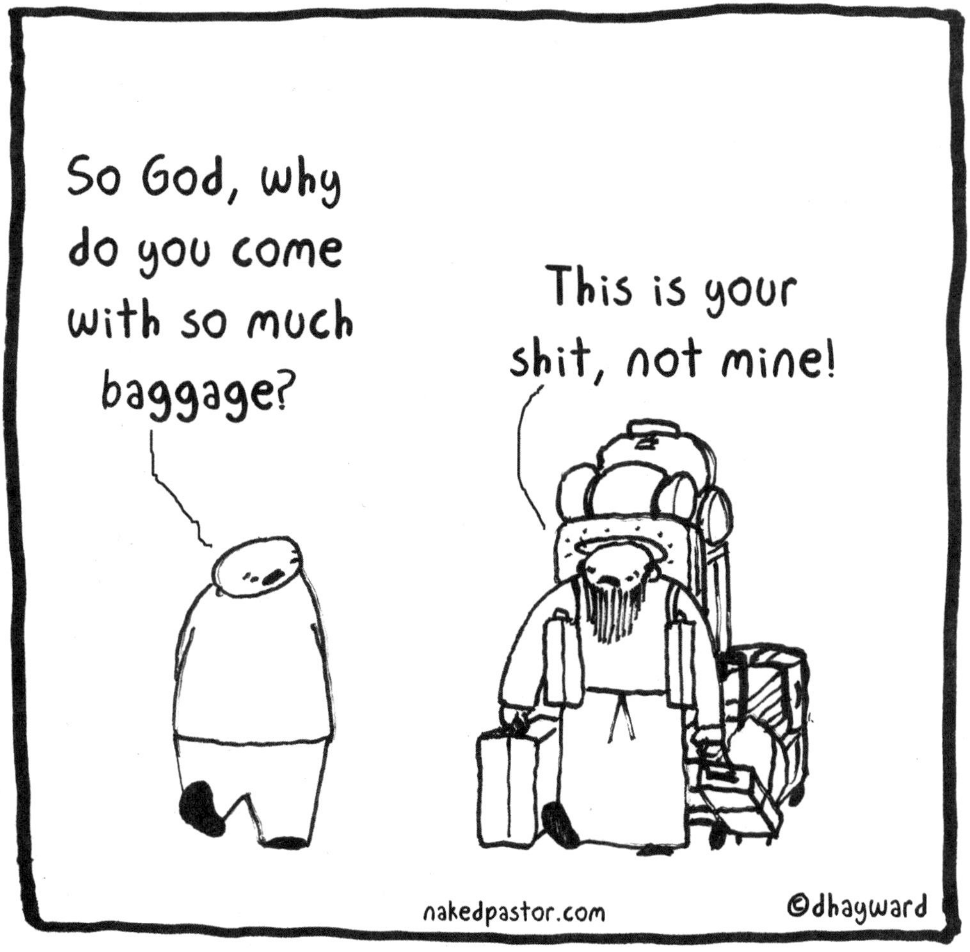
So God, why do you come with so much baggage?
This is your shit, not mine!
nakedpastor.com
©dhayward

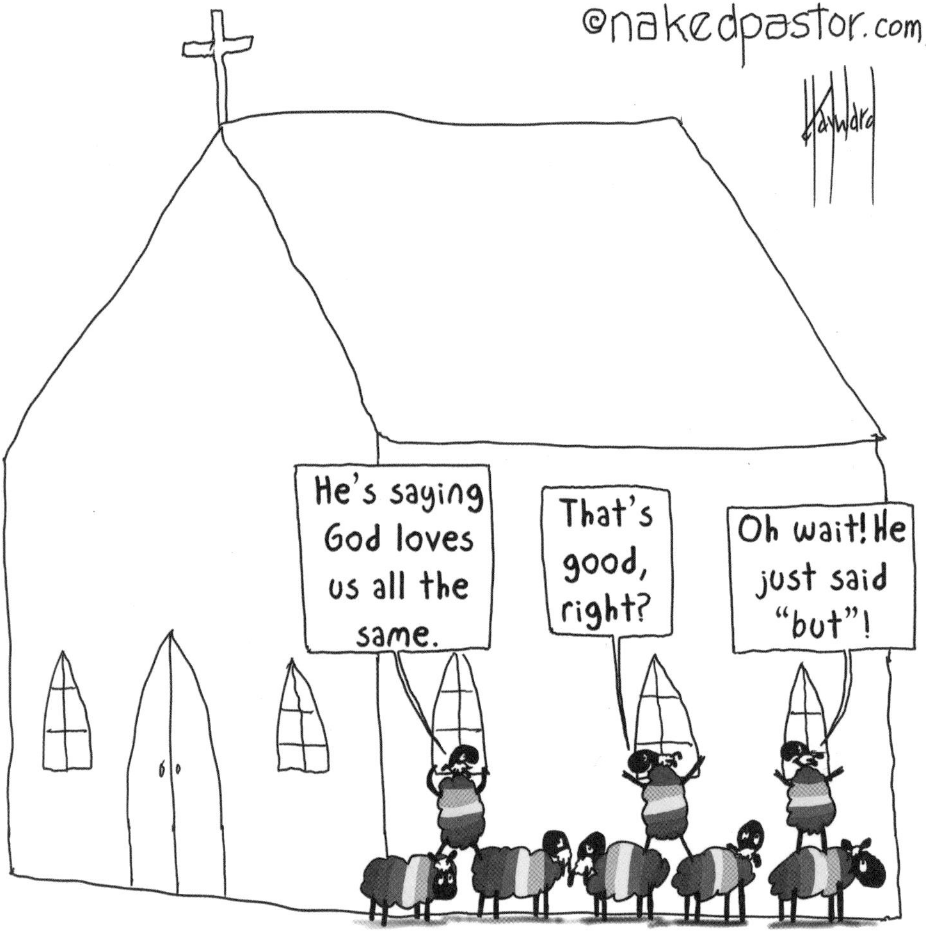
©nakedpastor.com
Hayward
He's saying God loves us all the same.
That's good, right?
Oh wait! He just said "but"!

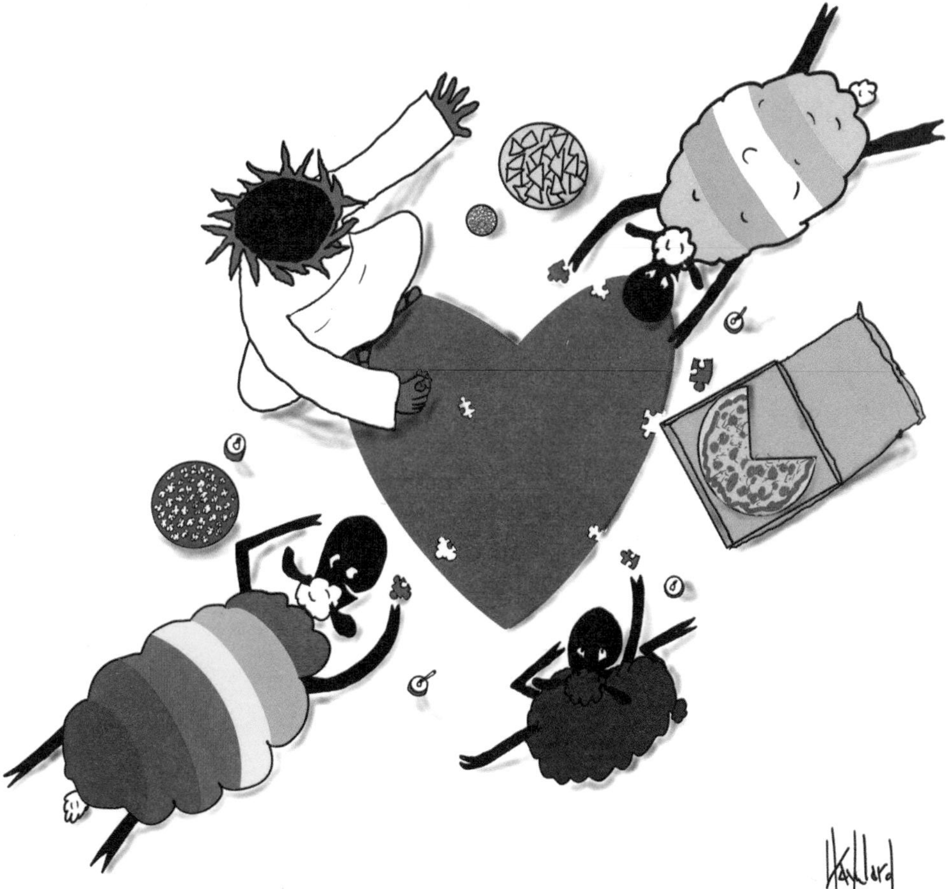
@nakedpastor.com

© nakedpastor.com
God loves you but ______.
THIS
CANCELS
THAT

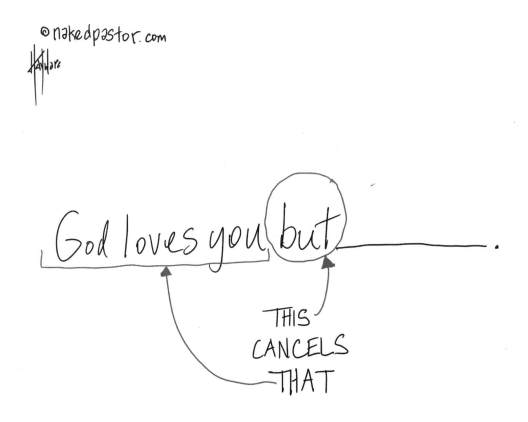

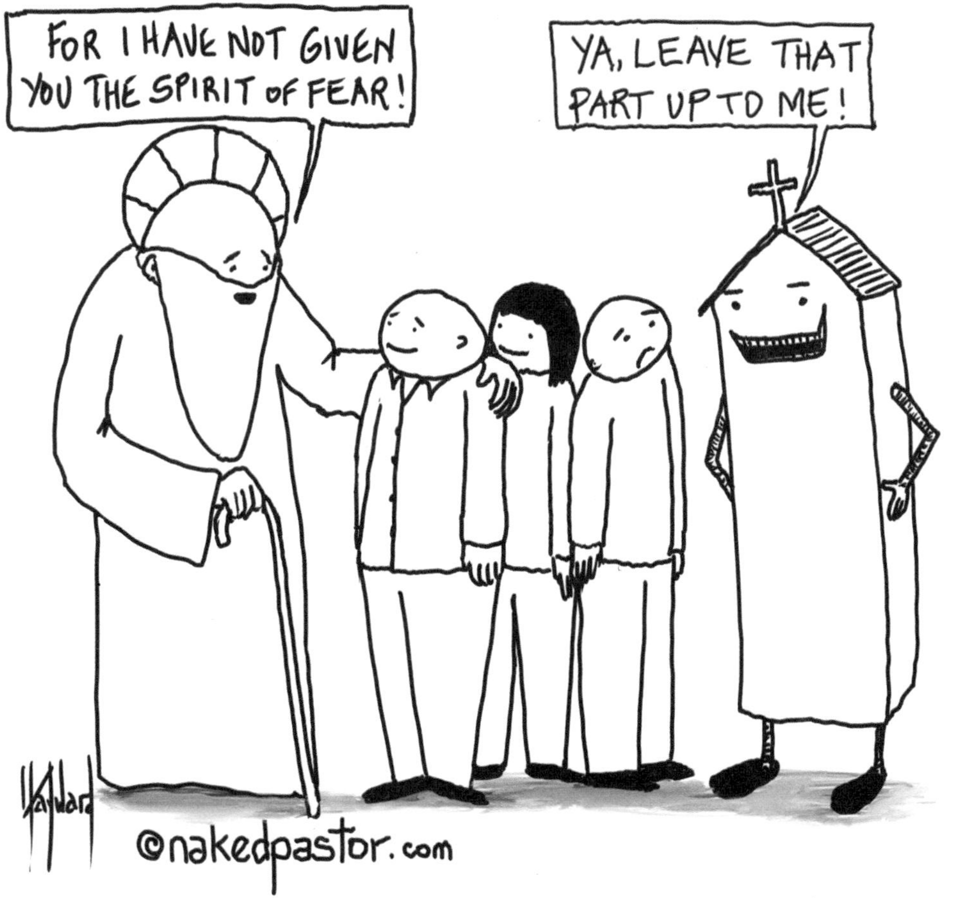
FOR I HAVE NOT GIVEN YOU THE SPIRIT OF FEAR!
YA, LEAVE THAT PART UP TO ME!
Hayward
©nakedpastor.com

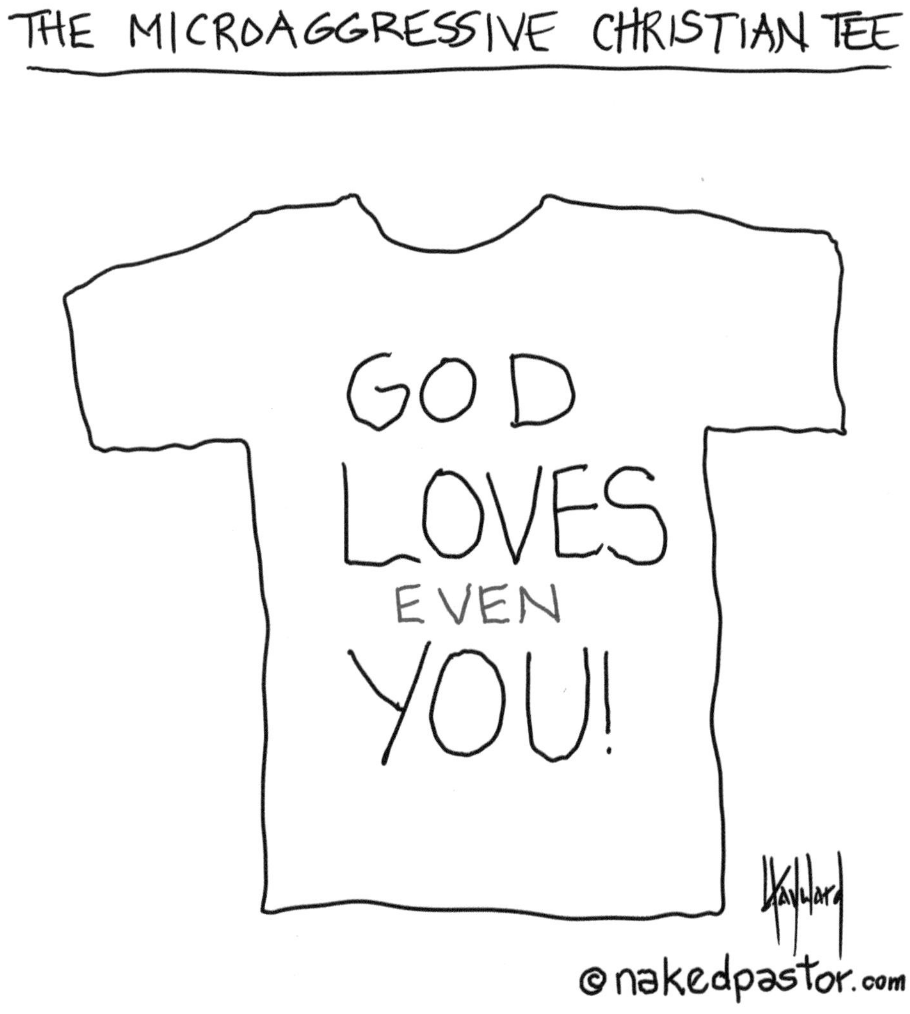
THE MICROAGGRESSIVE CHRISTIAN TEE
GOD
LOVES
EVEN
YOU!
Hayward
©nakedpastor.com

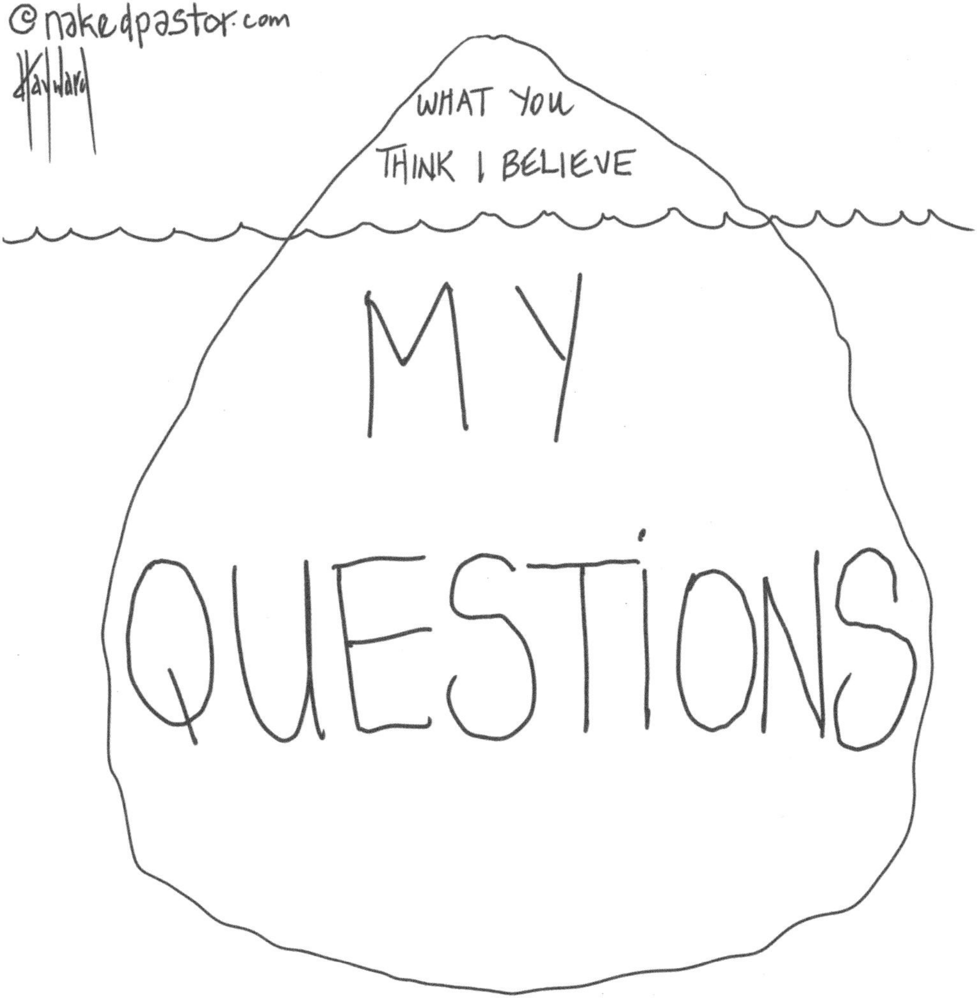
©nakedpastor.com
Hayward
WHAT YOU
THINK I BELIEVE
MY
QUESTIONS

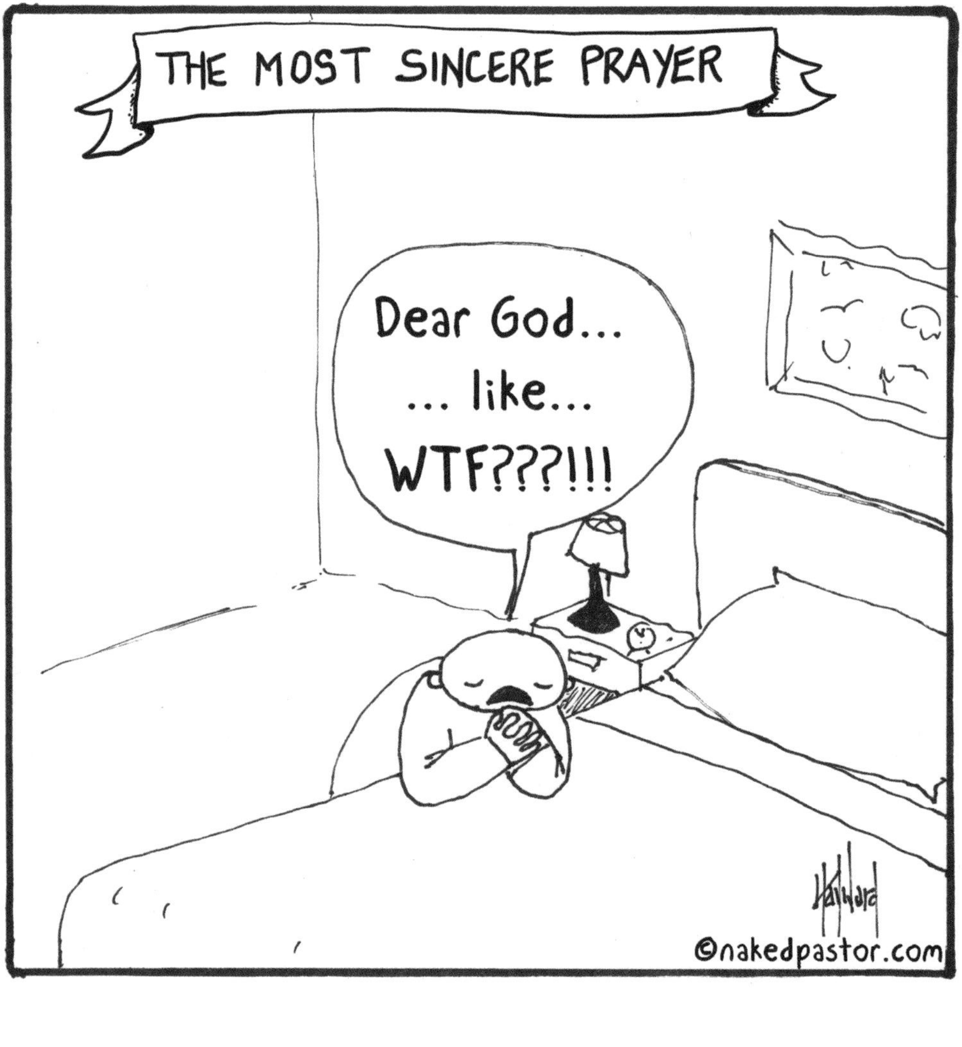
THE MOST SINCERE PRAYER
Dear God...
... like...
WTF???!!!
Hayward
©nakedpastor.com

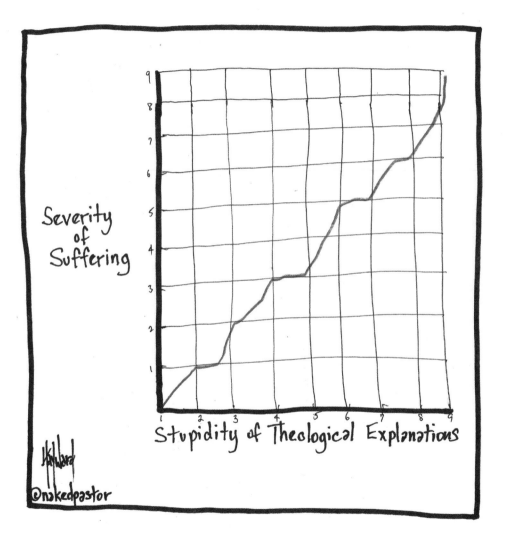

Severity of Suffering

Stupidity of Theological Explanations

@nakedpastor

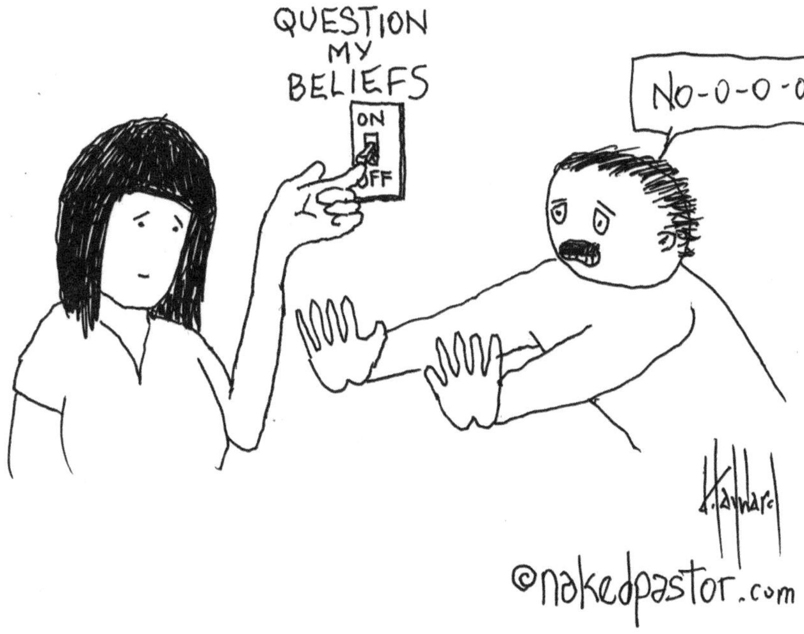
QUESTION MY BELIEFS
ON
OFF
No-o-o-o-o-o-o!
©nakedpastor.com

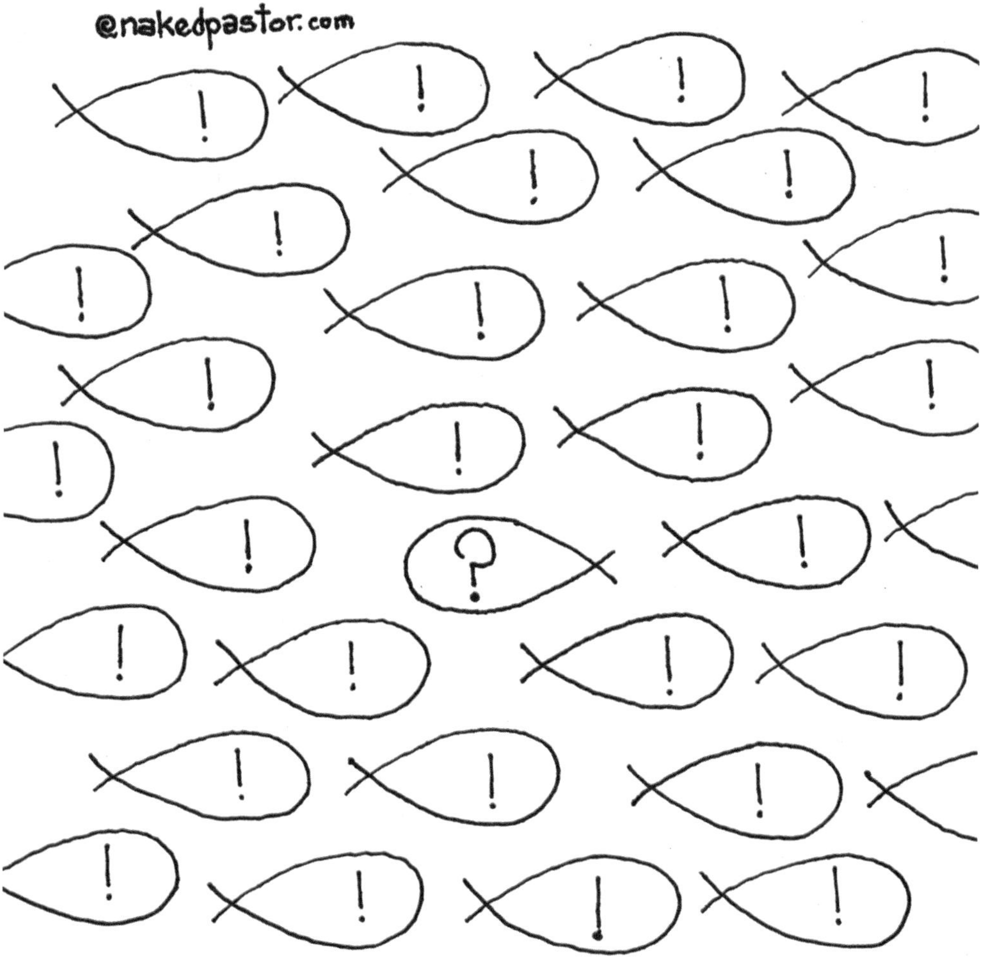
@nakedpastor.com

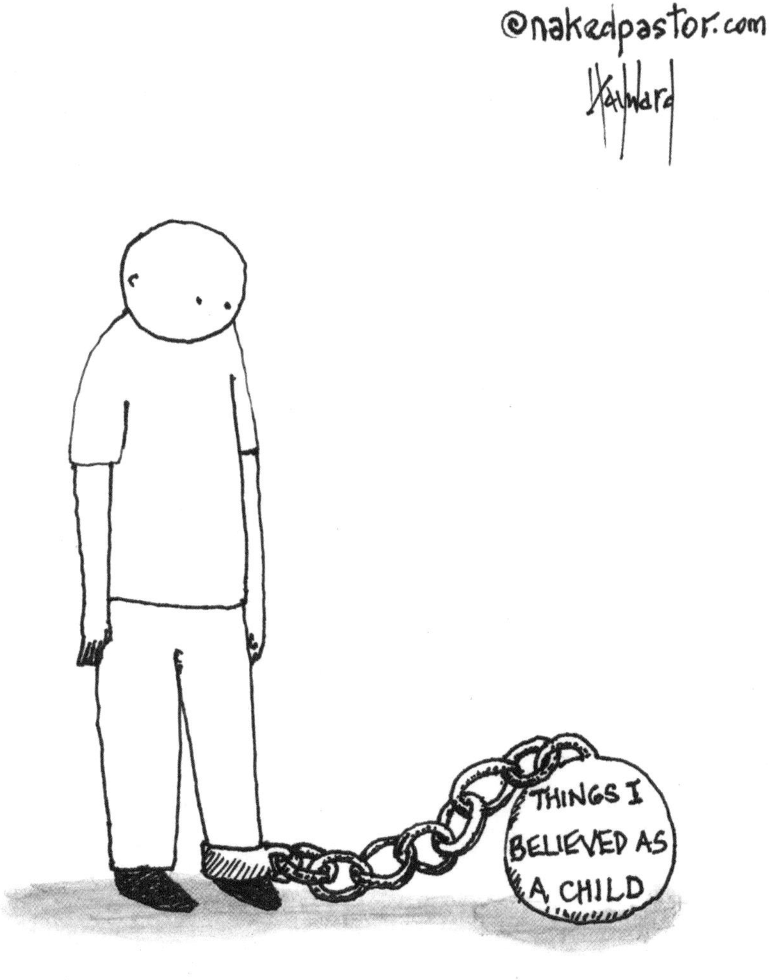

©nakedpastor.com
Hayward
THINGS I BELIEVED AS A CHILD

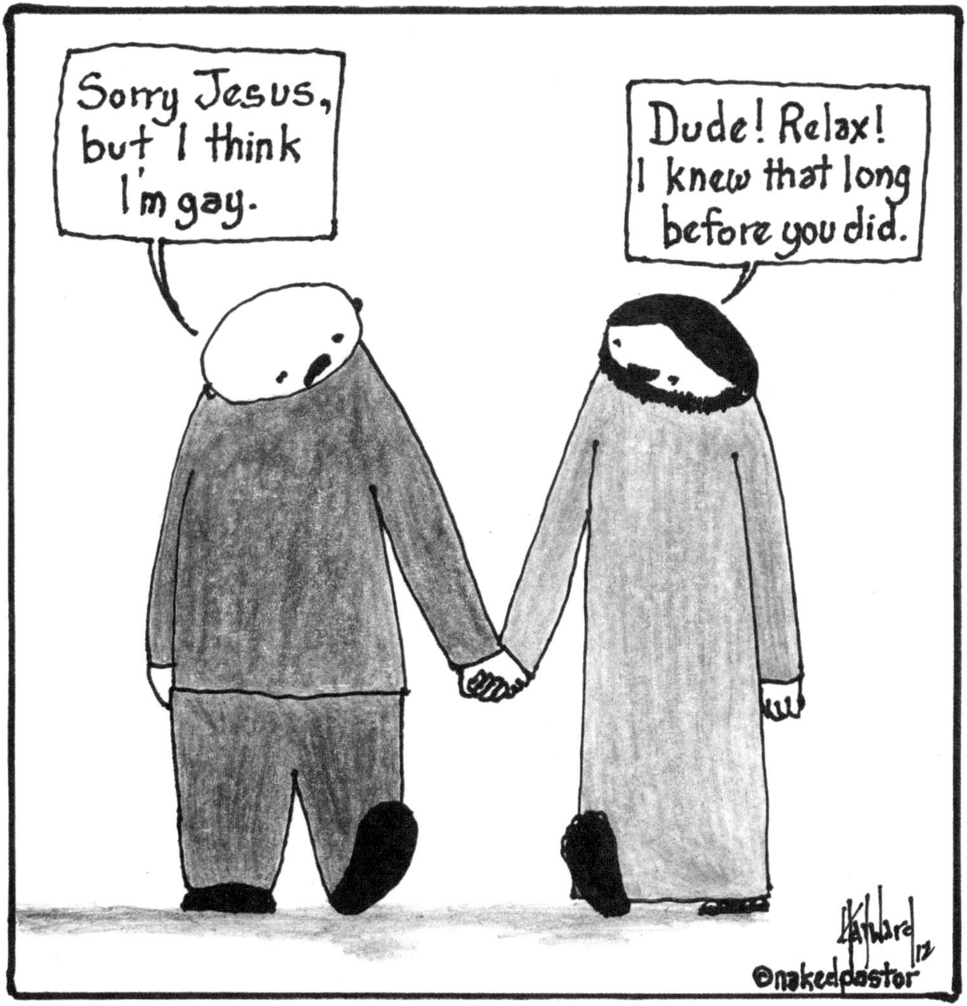
Sorry Jesus, but I think I'm gay.
Dude! Relax! I knew that long before you did.
Hayward 12
©nakedpastor

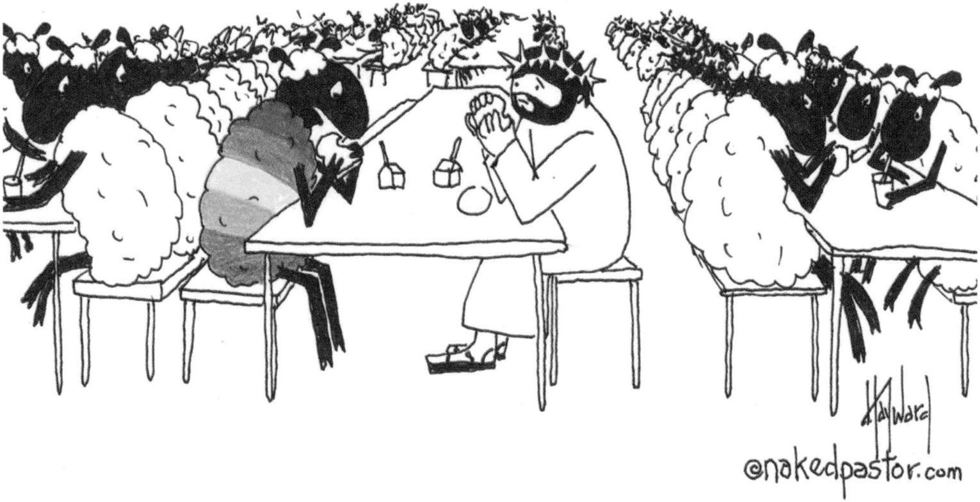
Hayward
©nakedpastor.com

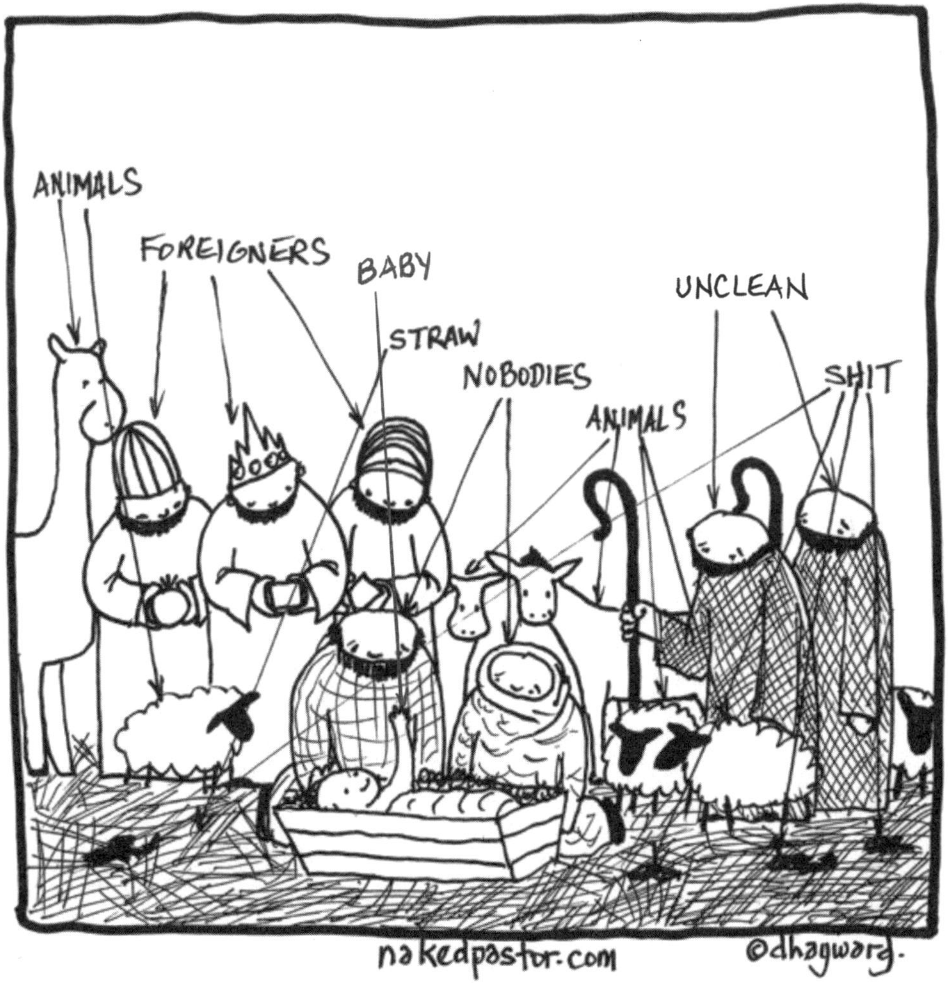
ANIMALS
FOREIGNERS
BABY
STRAW
NOBODIES
ANIMALS
UNCLEAN
SHIT
nakedpastor.com
©dhayward

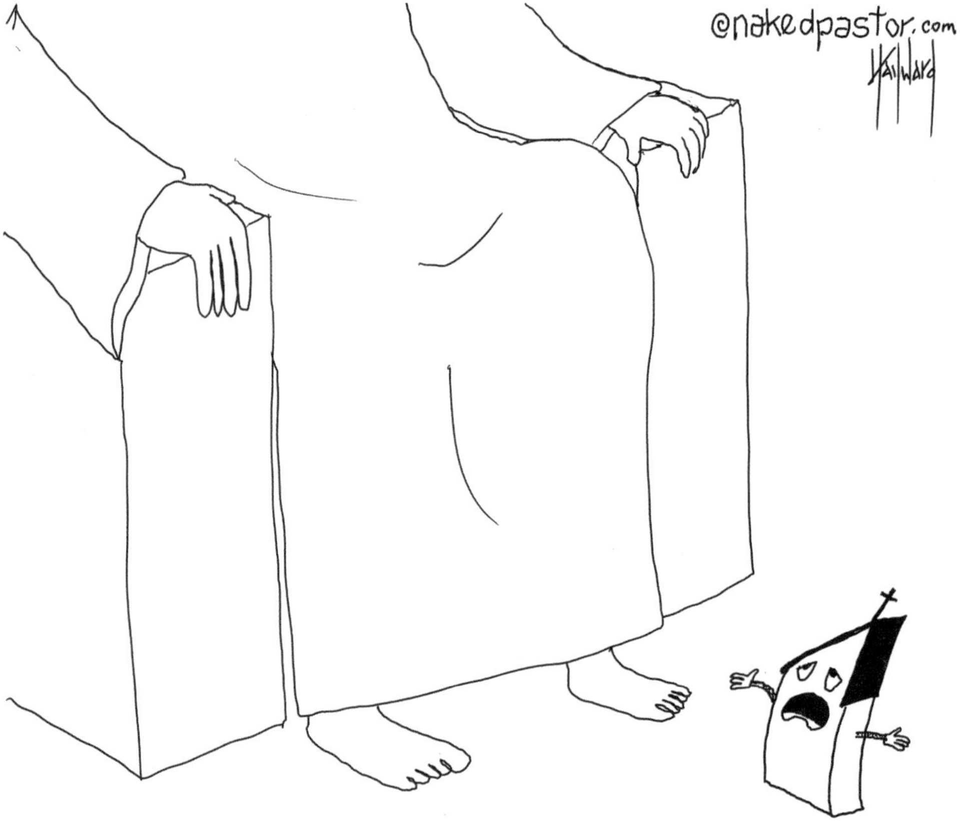
©nakedpastor.com
Hayward

"WHAT DO YOU MEAN WE NEVER SERVED THE POOR?!
WE DIDN'T KNOW ANY!!!"

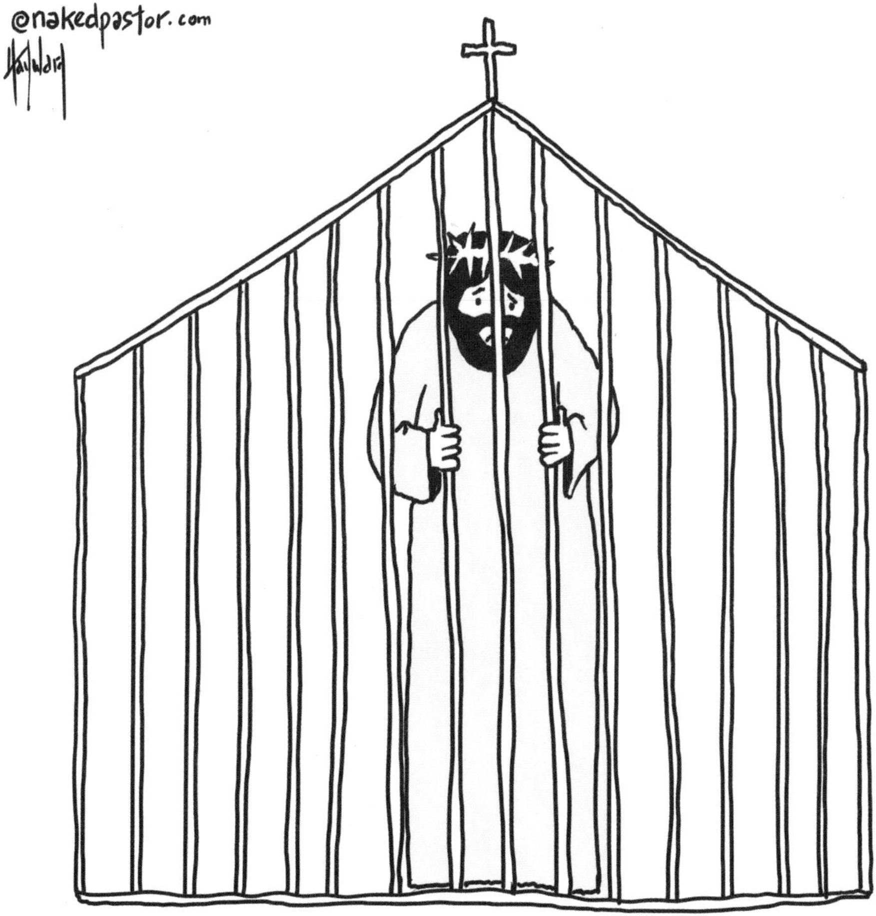
@nakedpastor.com
Hayward

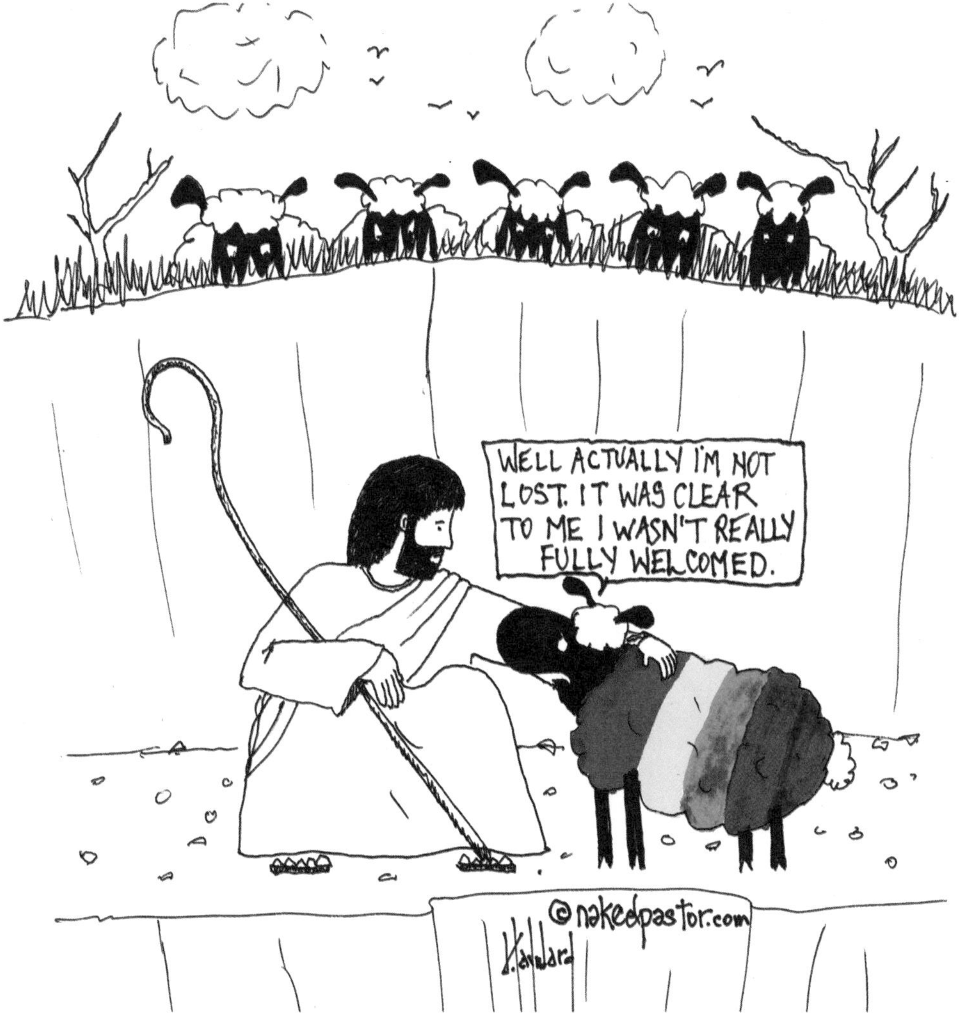
WELL ACTUALLY I'M NOT LOST. IT WAS CLEAR TO ME I WASN'T REALLY FULLY WELCOMED.
©nakedpastor.com

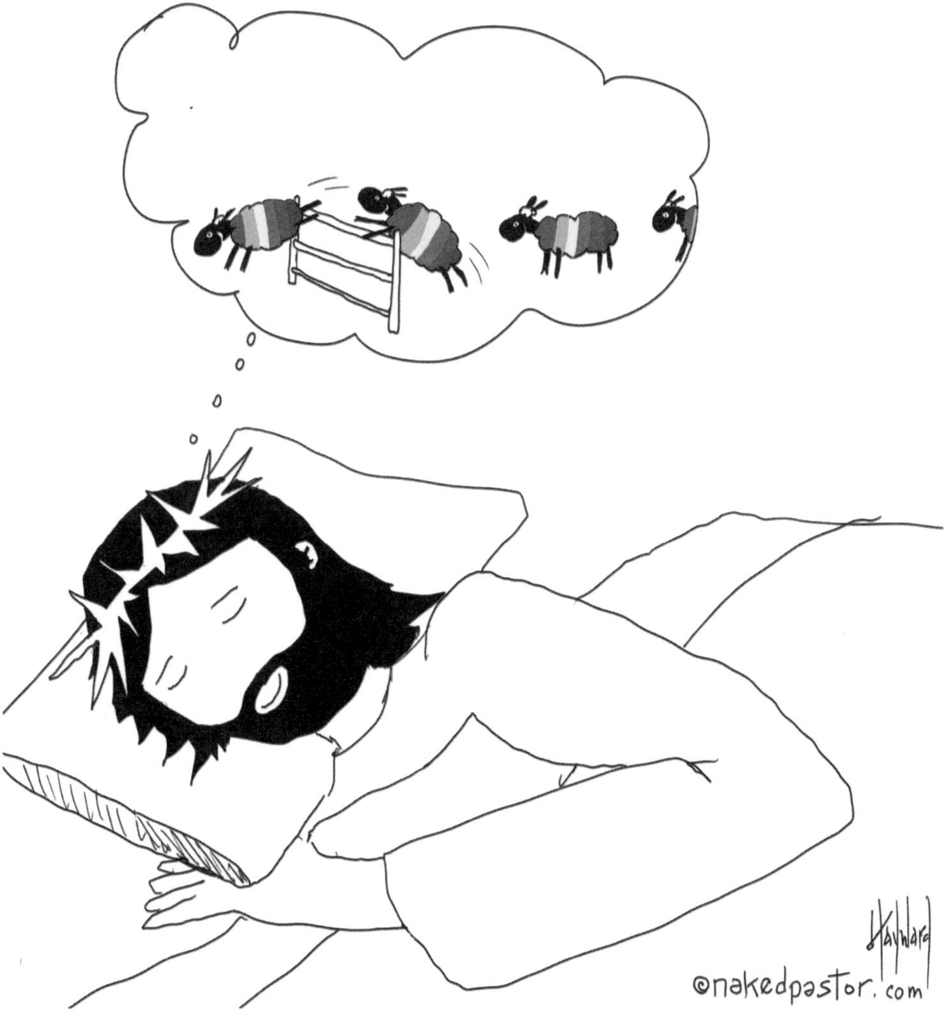
Hayward
©nakedpastor.com

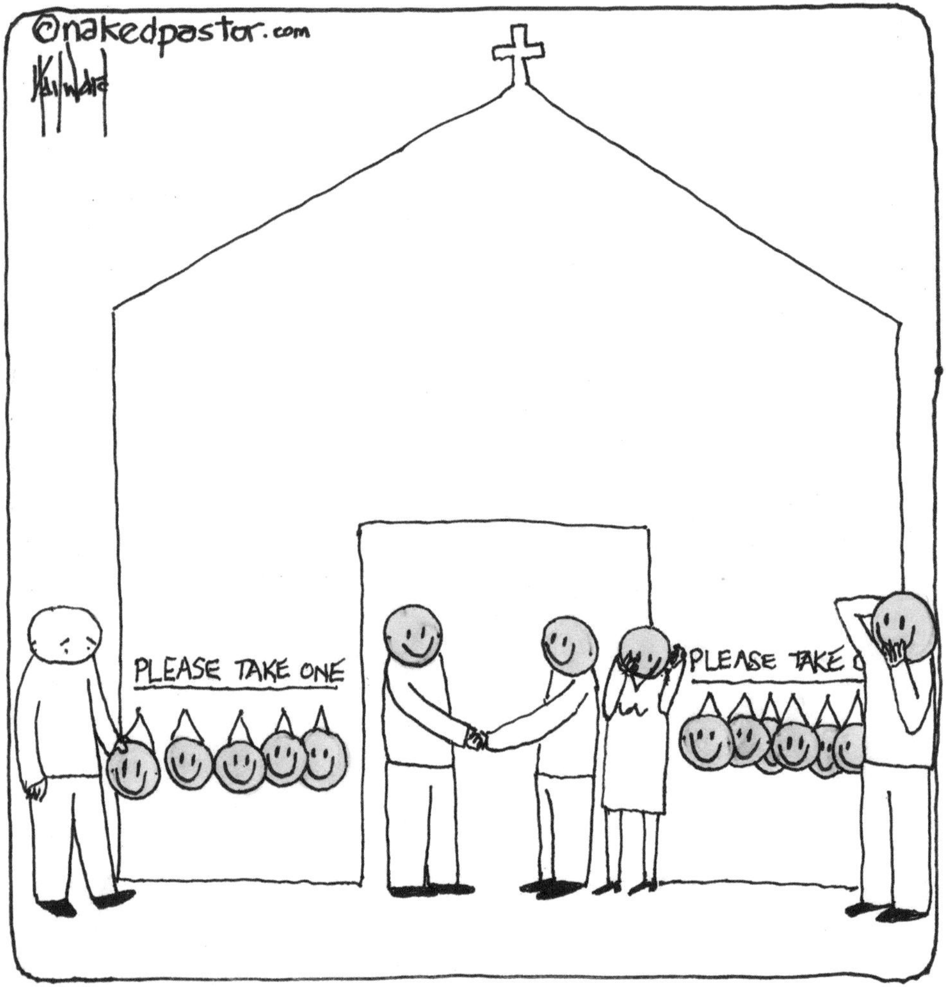
©nakedpastor.com
PLEASE TAKE ONE
PLEASE TAKE

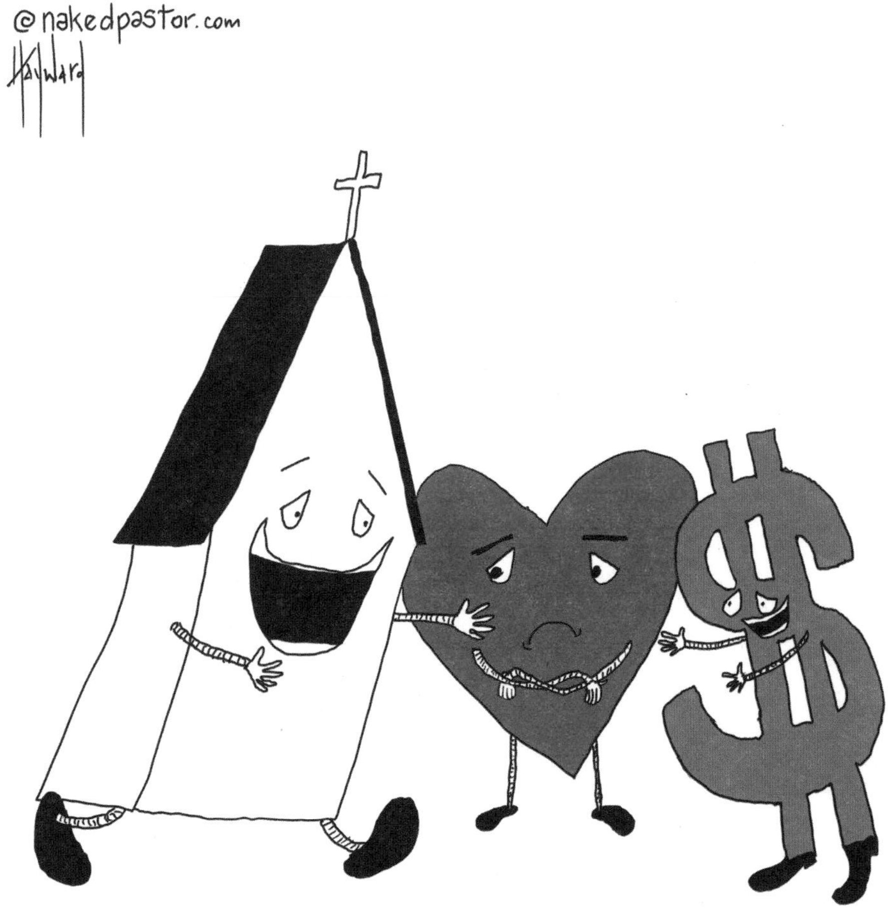
@nakedpastor.com
Hayward

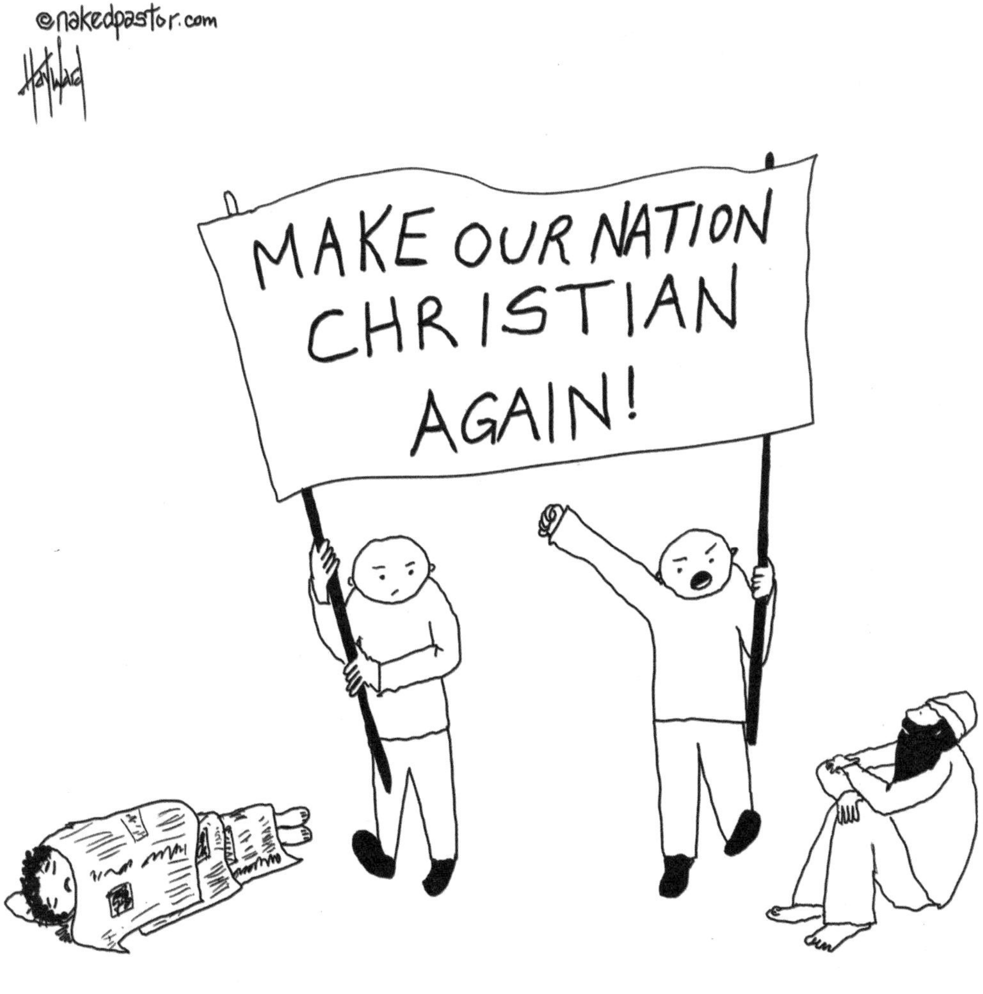

©nakedpastor.com
Hayward
MAKE OUR NATION
CHRISTIAN
AGAIN!

©nakedpastor.com
CHURCH
STATE
= ASSHOLERY

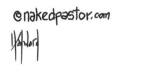

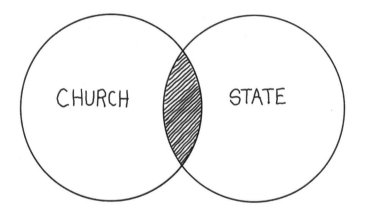

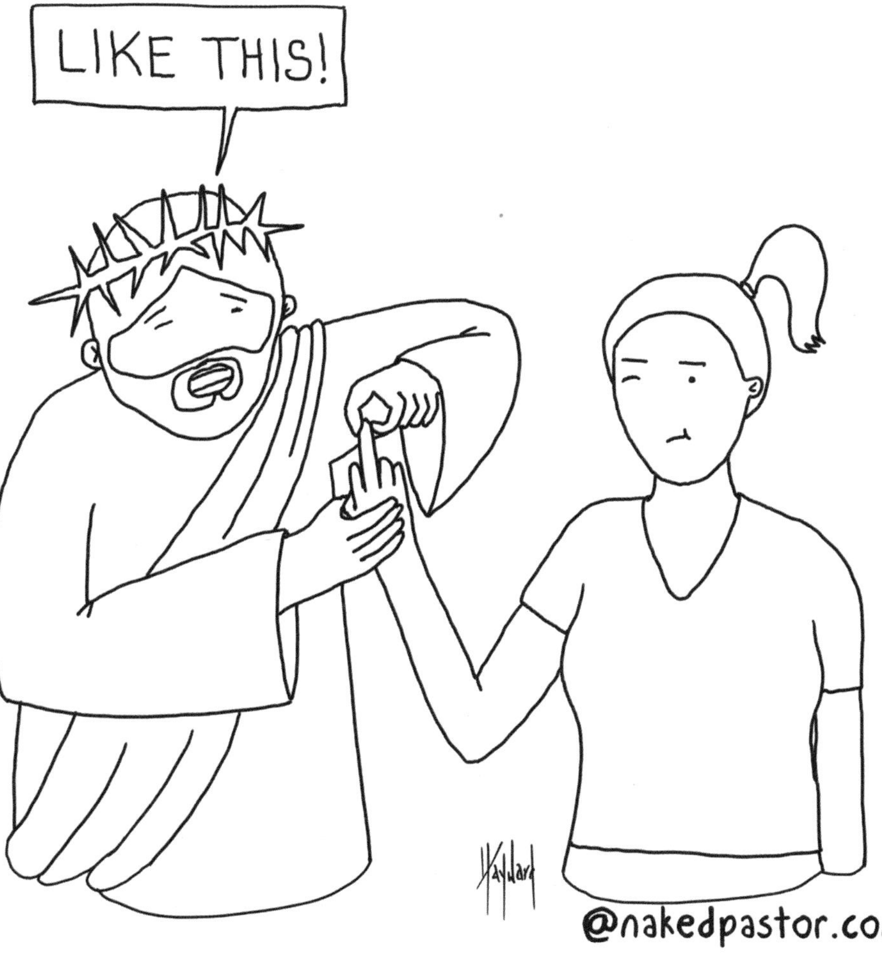
LIKE THIS!
@nakedpastor.com

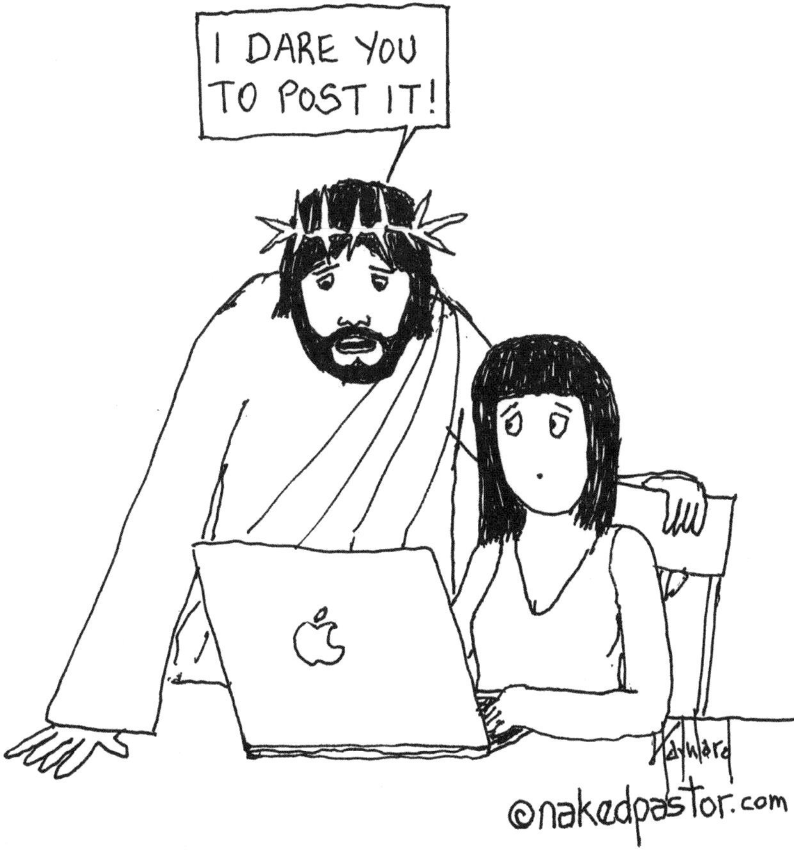
I DARE YOU TO POST IT!
Hayward
©nakedpastor.com

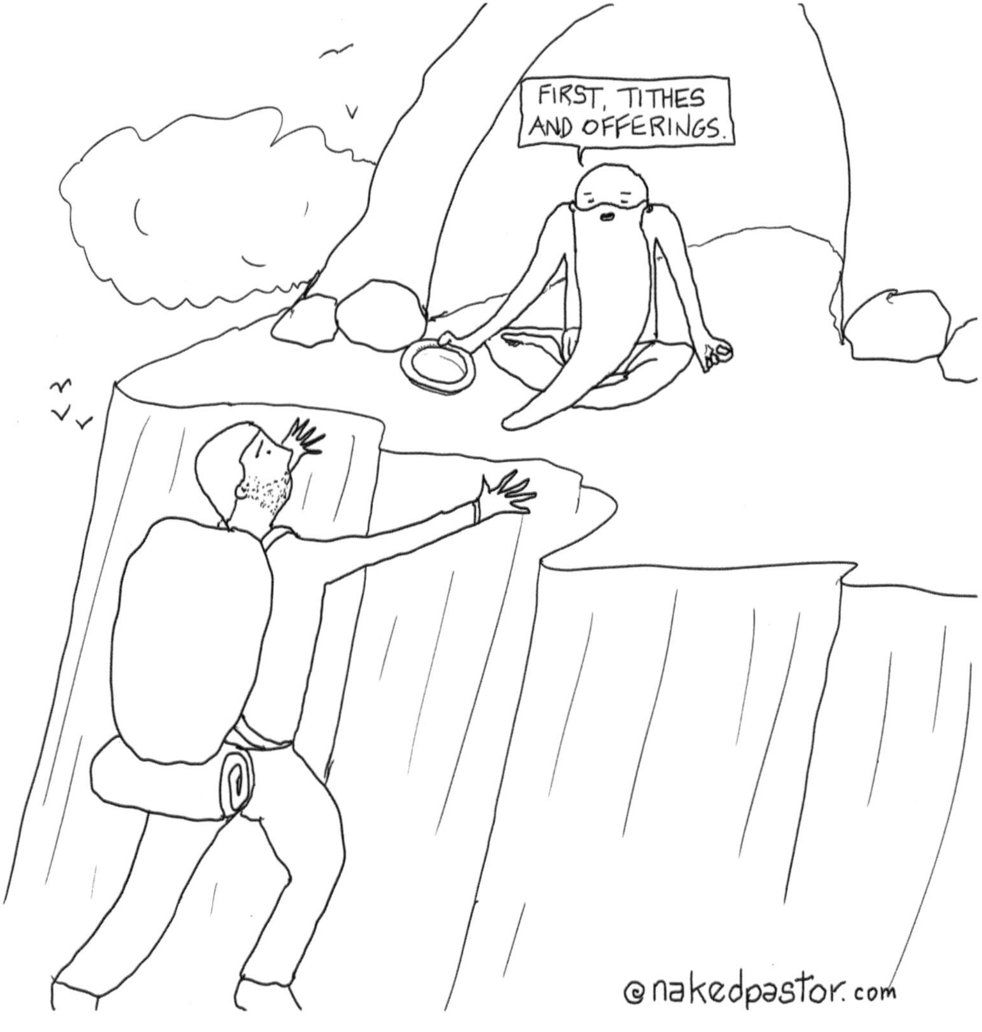
FIRST, TITHES AND OFFERINGS.
©nakedpastor.com

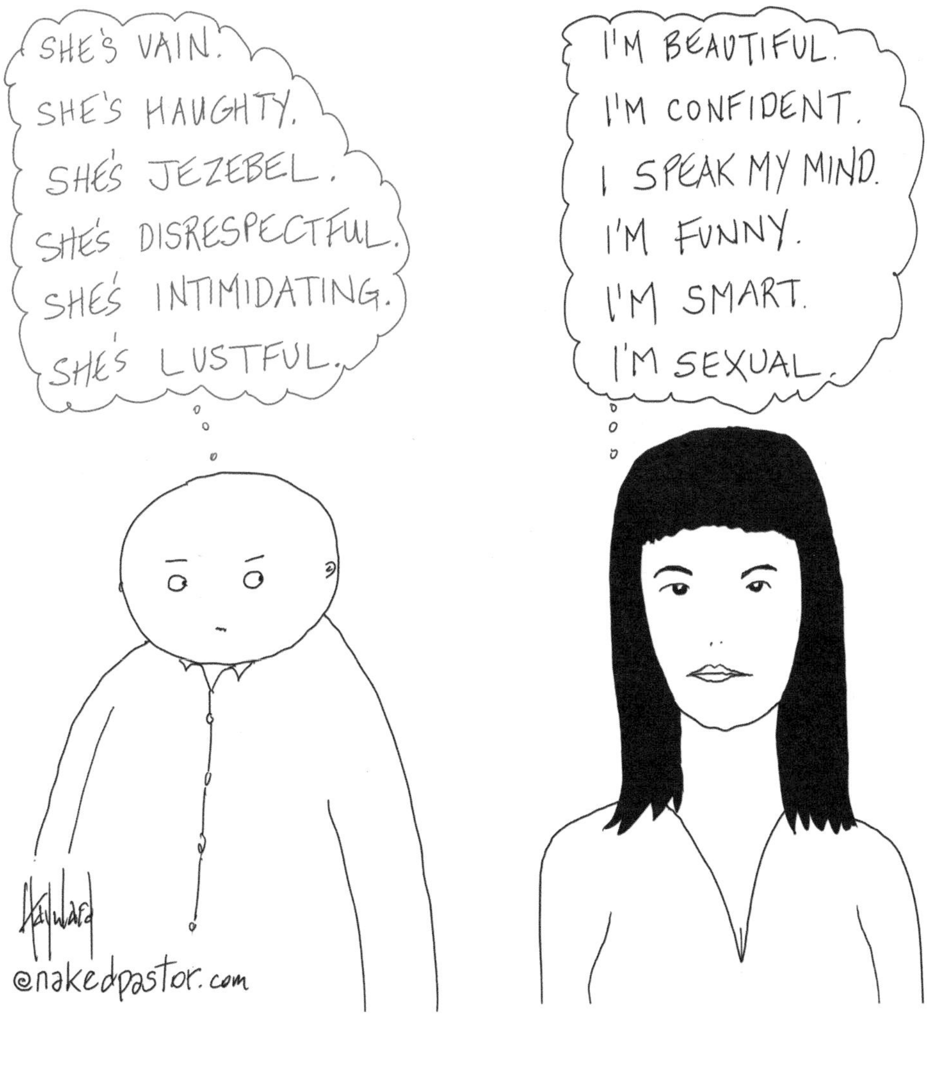
SHE'S VAIN.
SHE'S HAUGHTY.
SHE'S JEZEBEL.
SHE'S DISRESPECTFUL.
SHE'S INTIMIDATING.
SHE'S LUSTFUL.
I'M BEAUTIFUL.
I'M CONFIDENT.
I SPEAK MY MIND.
I'M FUNNY.
I'M SMART.
I'M SEXUAL.
@nakedpastor.com

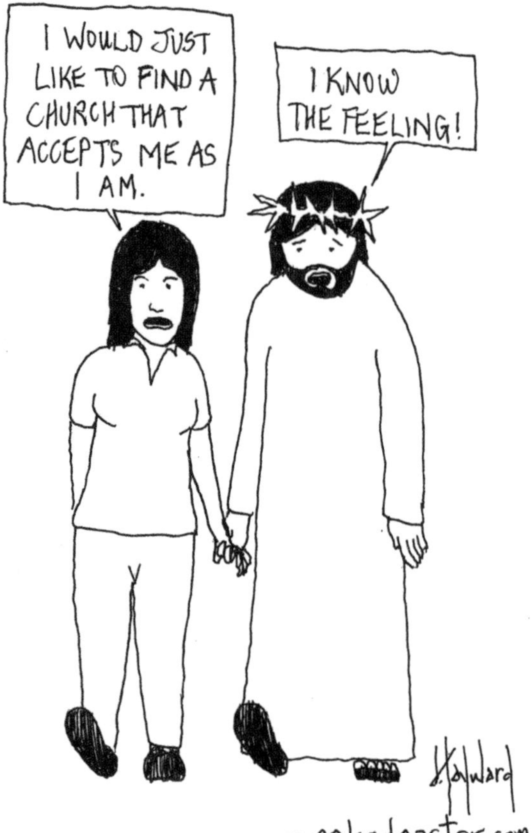
I WOULD JUST LIKE TO FIND A CHURCH THAT ACCEPTS ME AS I AM.
I KNOW THE FEELING!
©nakedpastor.com

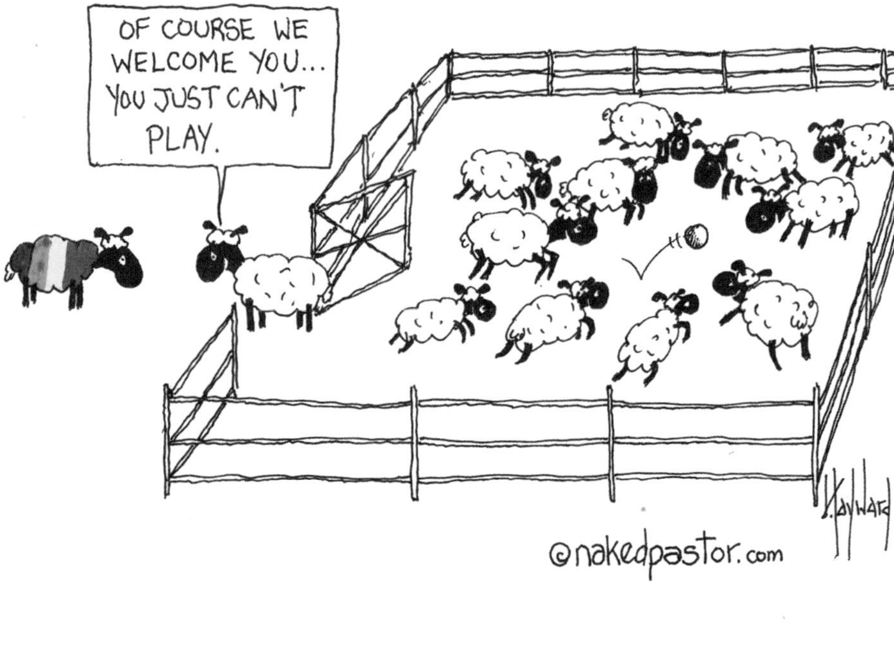
OF COURSE WE WELCOME YOU... YOU JUST CAN'T PLAY.
Hayward
©nakedpastor.com

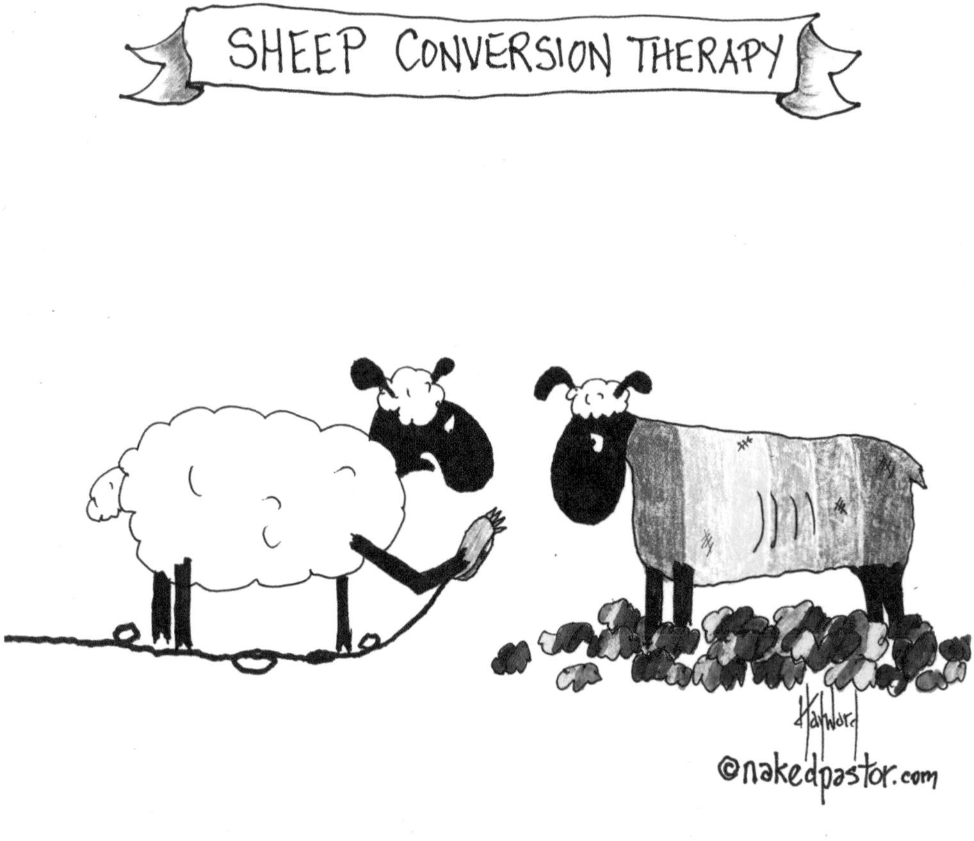
SHEEP CONVERSION THERAPY
Hayward
©nakedpastor.com

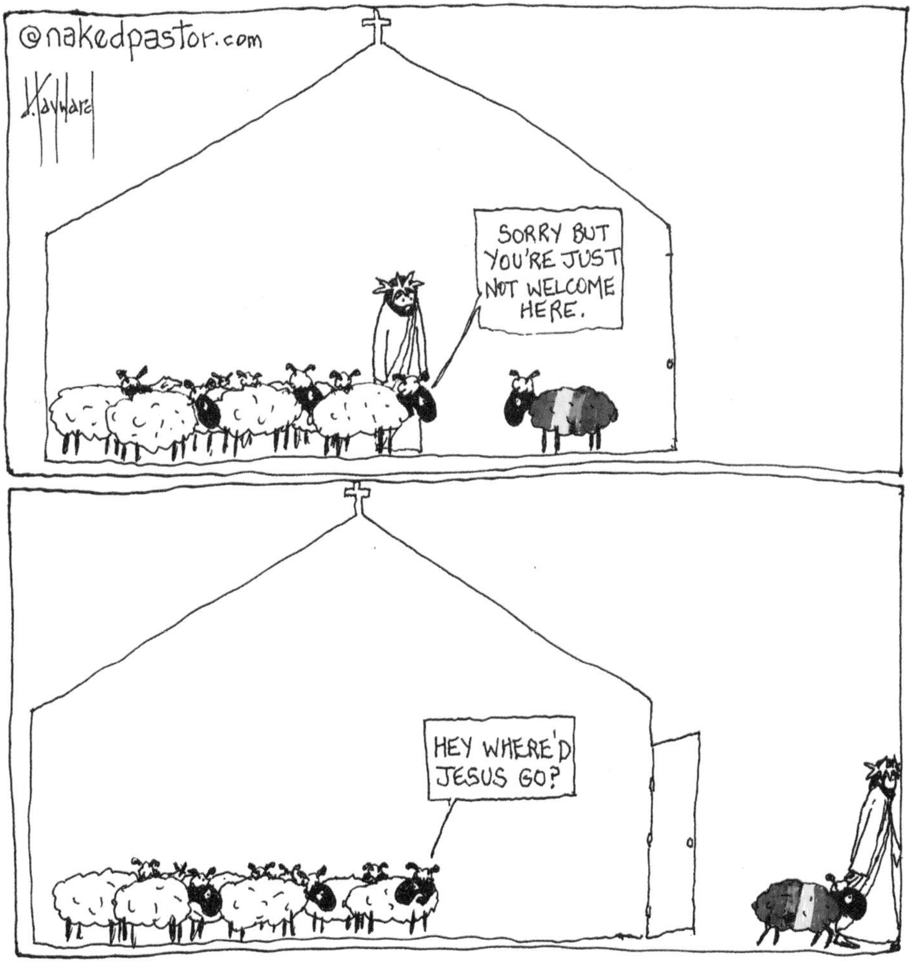
@nakedpastor.com
D.Hayward
SORRY BUT YOU'RE JUST NOT WELCOME HERE.
HEY WHERE'D JESUS GO?

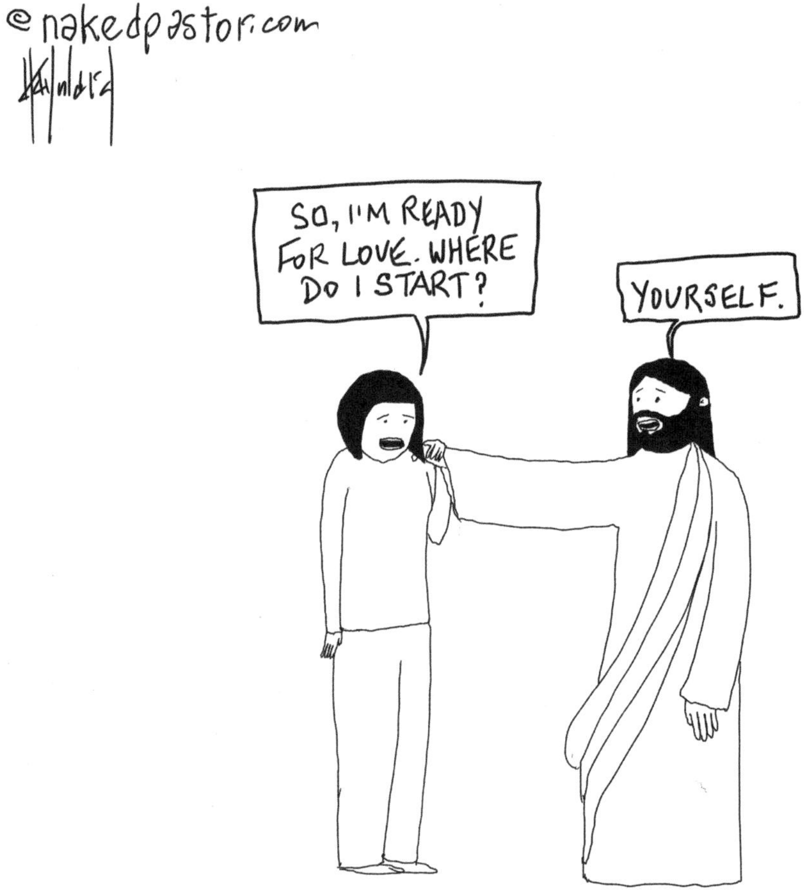
©nakedpastor.com
SO, I'M READY FOR LOVE. WHERE DO I START?
YOURSELF.

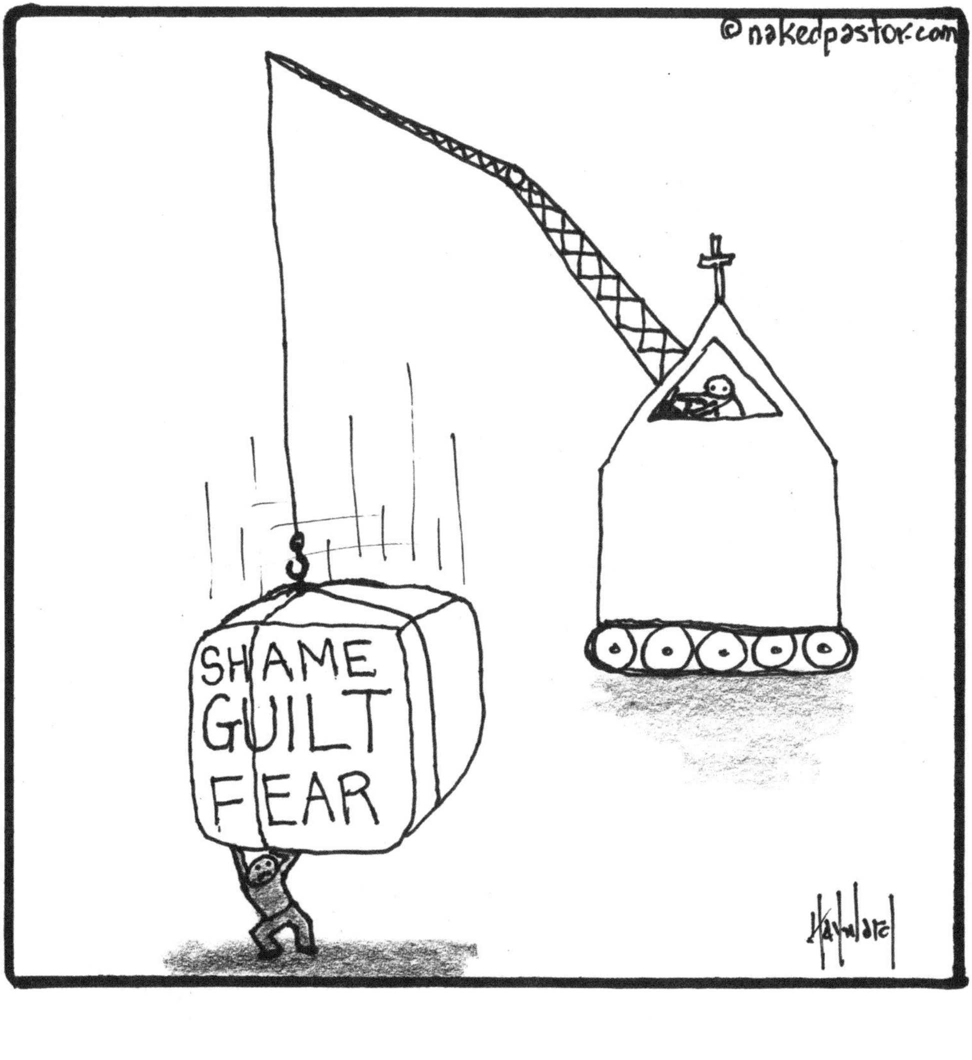
©nakedpastor.com
SHAME
GUILT
FEAR
Hayward

FIRST CHURCH
WELCOME

GOD LOVES YOU
~~JUST THE WAY YOU ARE~~
~~BUT HE LOVES YOU TOO MUCH~~
~~TO LEAVE YOU THAT WAY.~~

FIXED IT!

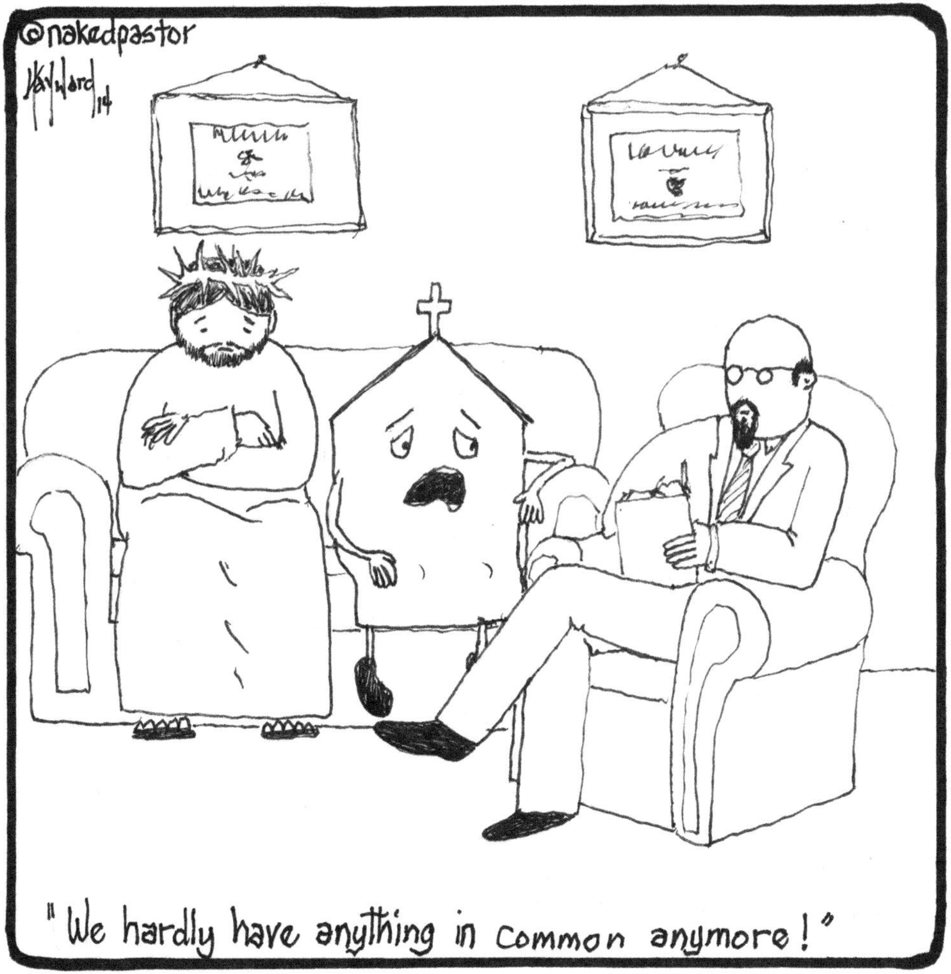
©nakedpastor
Hayward 14
"We hardly have anything in common anymore!"

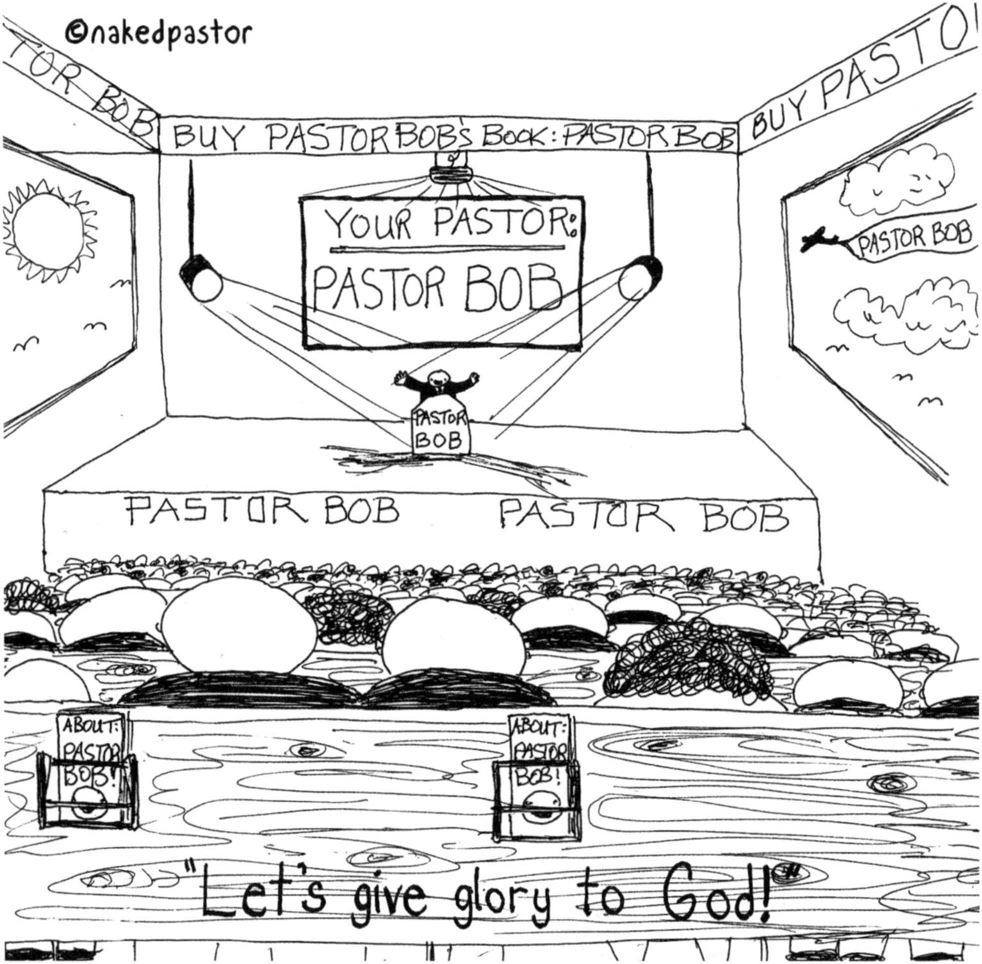
©nakedpastor
BUY PASTOR BOB's BOOK: PASTOR BOB
YOUR PASTOR:
PASTOR BOB
PASTOR BOB
PASTOR BOB
PASTOR BOB
PASTOR BOB
ABOUT: PASTOR BOB!
ABOUT: PASTOR BOB!
"Let's give glory to God!"

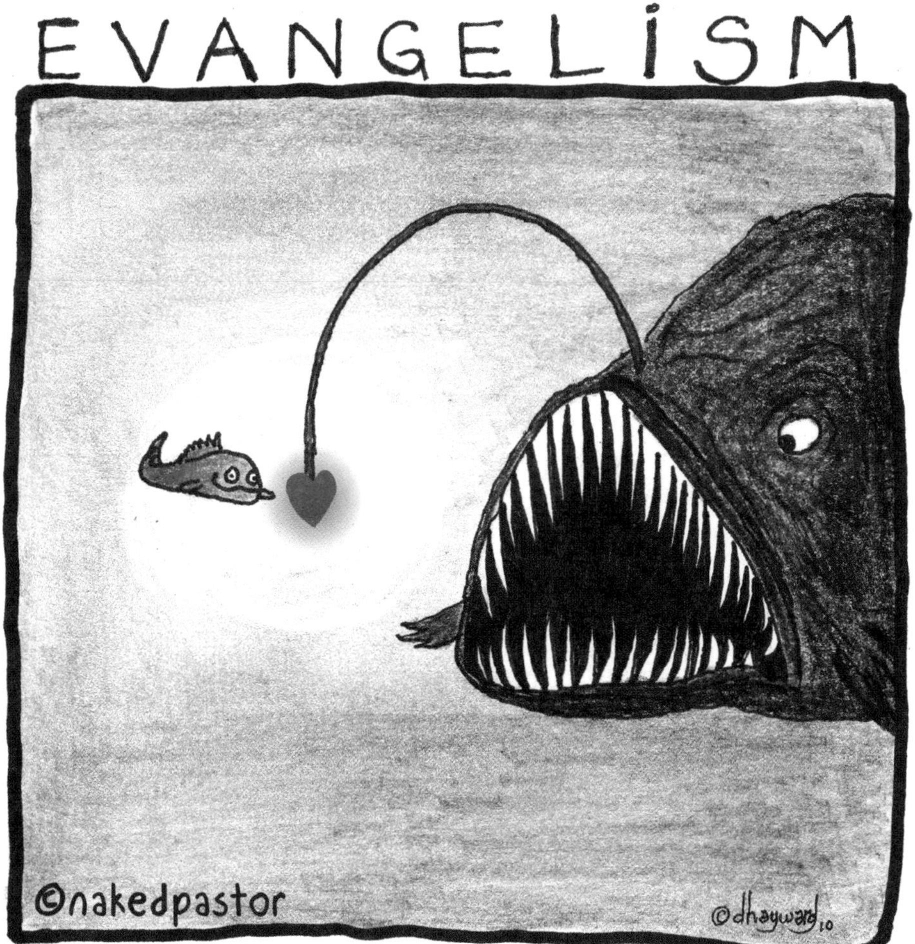
EVANGELISM
©nakedpastor
©dhayward10

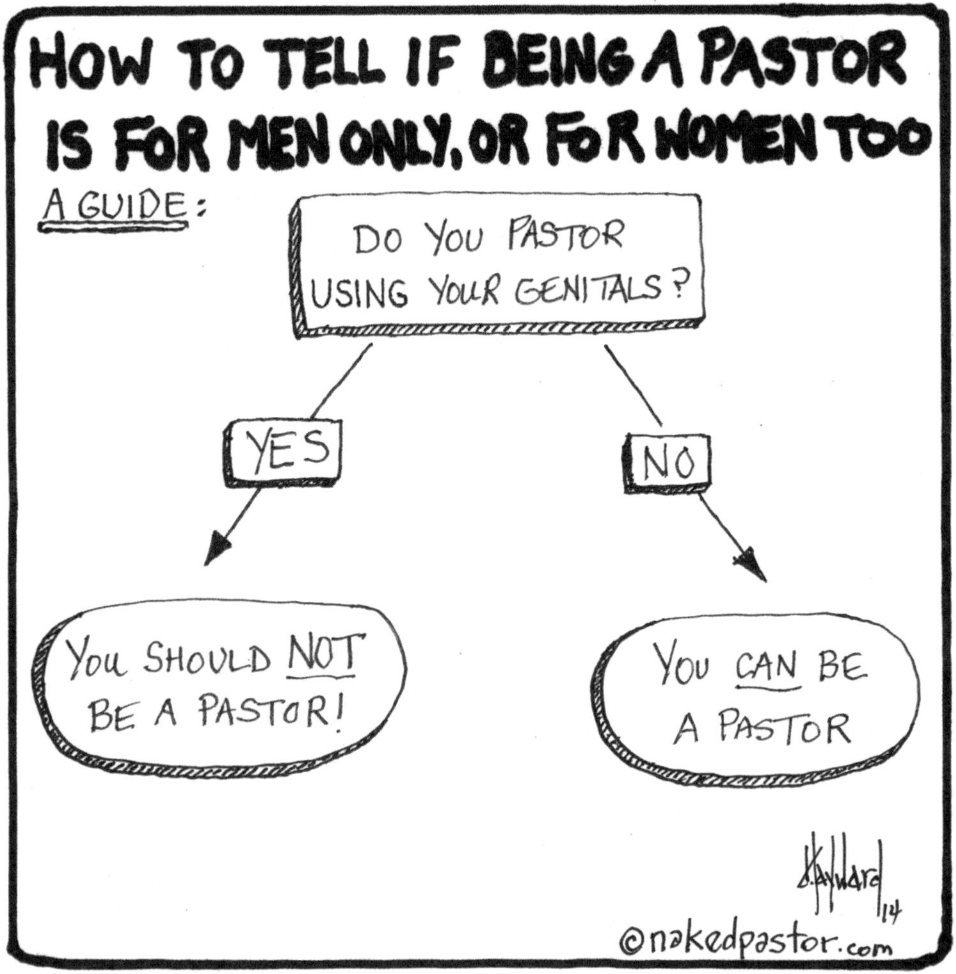
HOW TO TELL IF BEING A PASTOR IS FOR MEN ONLY, OR FOR WOMEN TOO
A GUIDE:
DO YOU PASTOR USING YOUR GENITALS?
YES
NO
YOU SHOULD NOT BE A PASTOR!
YOU CAN BE A PASTOR
©nakedpastor.com

@nakedpastor.com
Hayward
NOT MY CHURCH!
NOT ALL
NOT ALL CHURCHES
HARDLY EVER HAPPENS
SPIRITUAL ABUSE

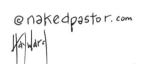

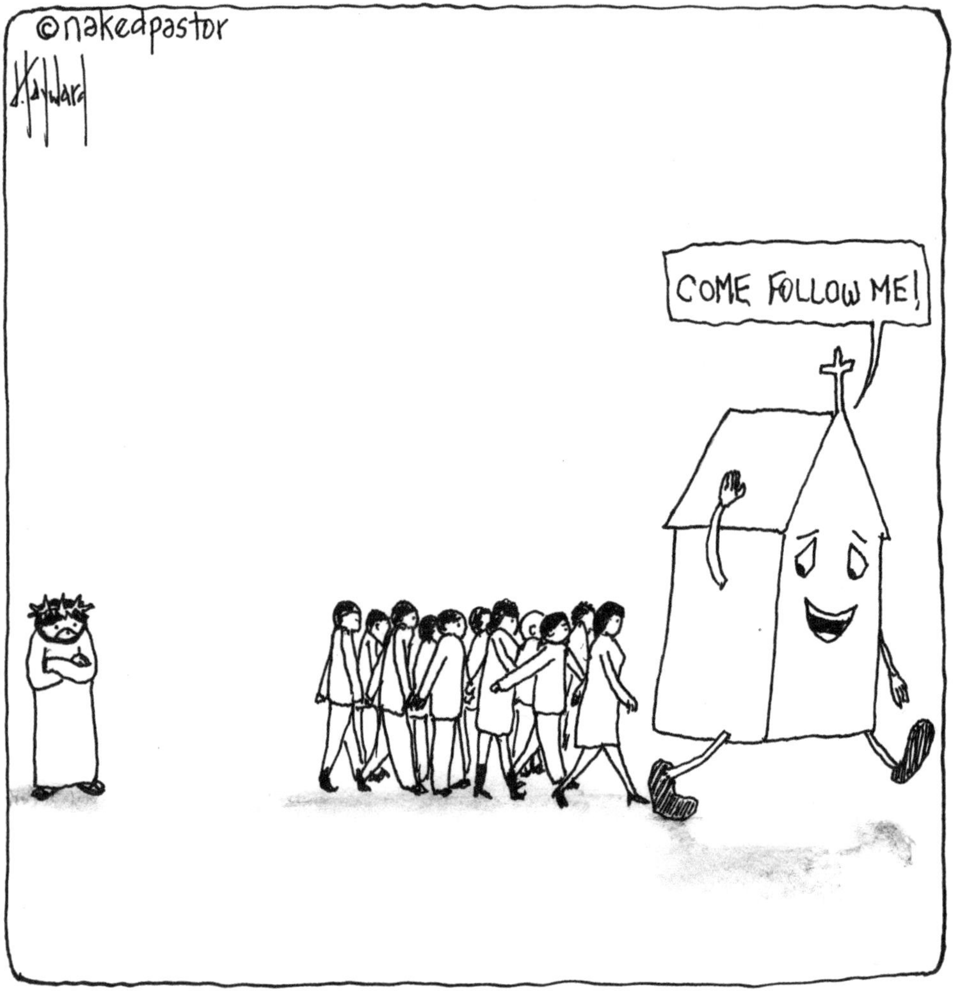
©nakedpastor
D.Hayward
COME FOLLOW ME!

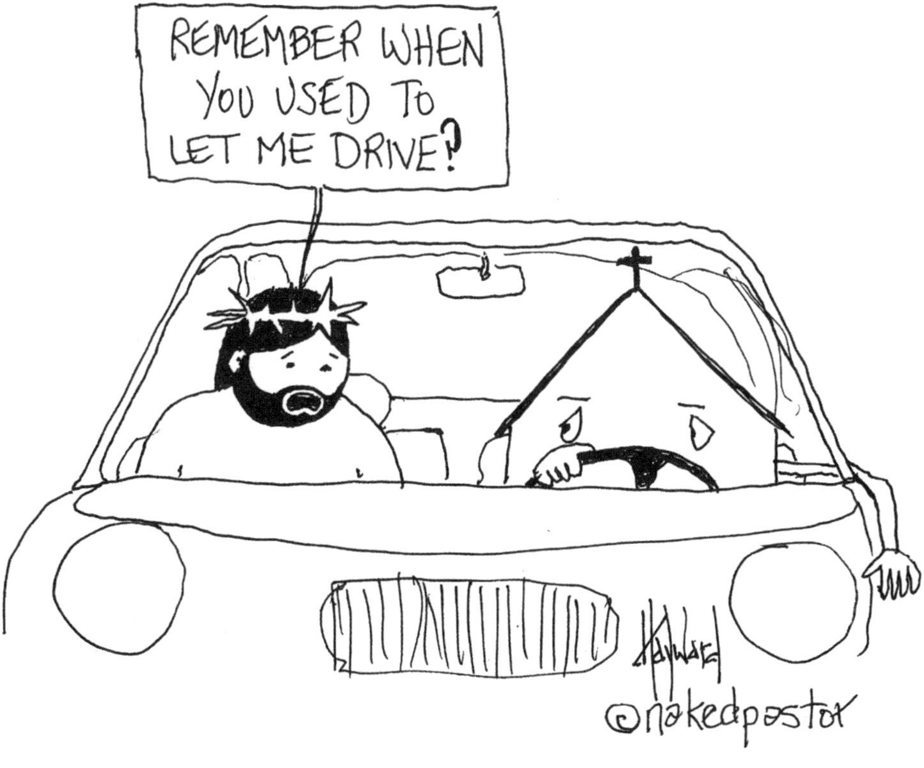
REMEMBER WHEN YOU USED TO LET ME DRIVE?
Hayward
©nakedpastor

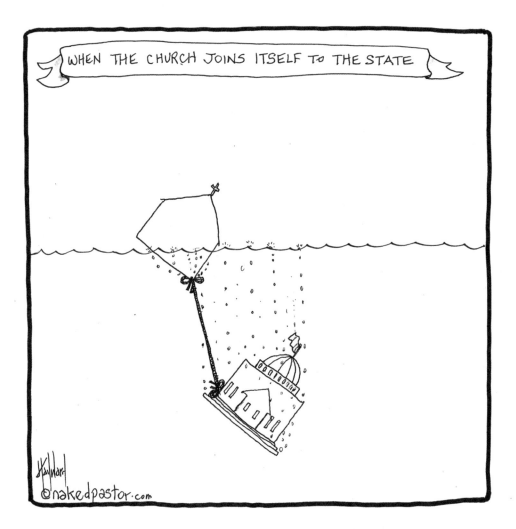

WHEN THE CHURCH JOINS ITSELF TO THE STATE

@nakedpastor.com

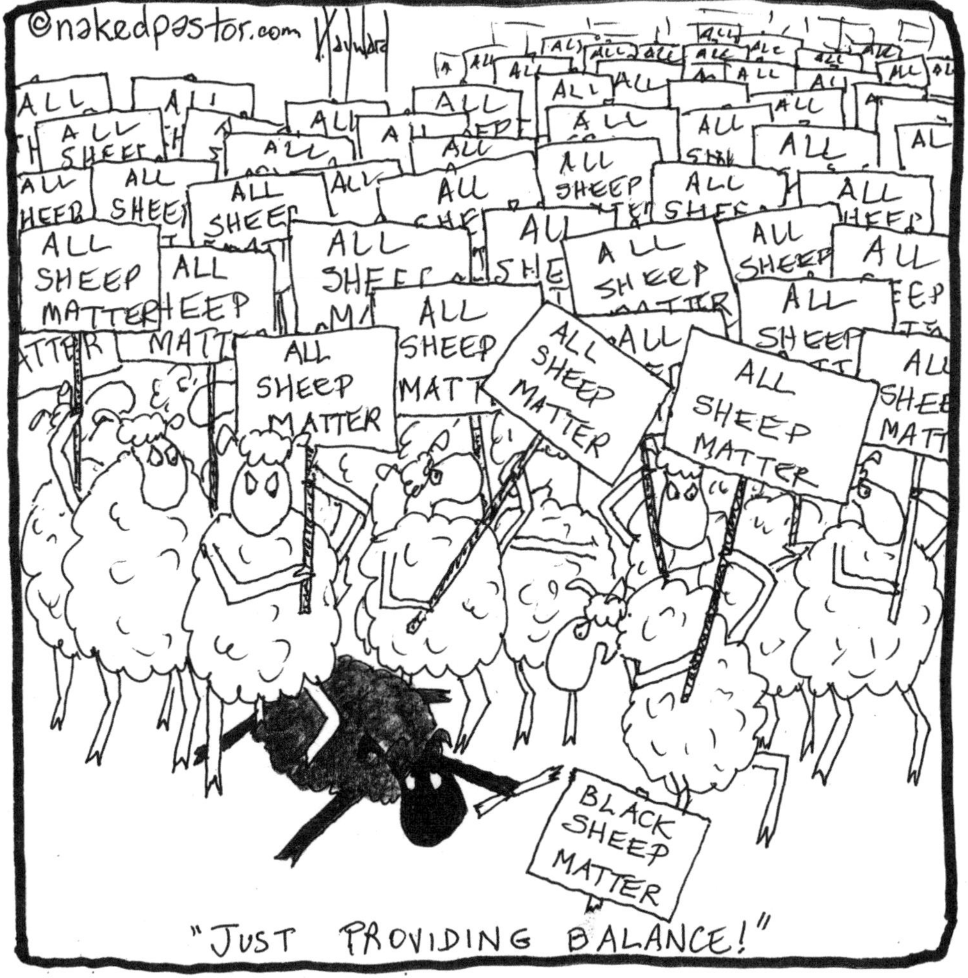
©nakedpastor.com
ALL SHEEP MATTER
ALL SHEEP MATTER
ALL SHEEP MATTER
ALL SHEEP MATTER
ALL SHEEP MATTER
BLACK SHEEP MATTER
"JUST PROVIDING BALANCE!"

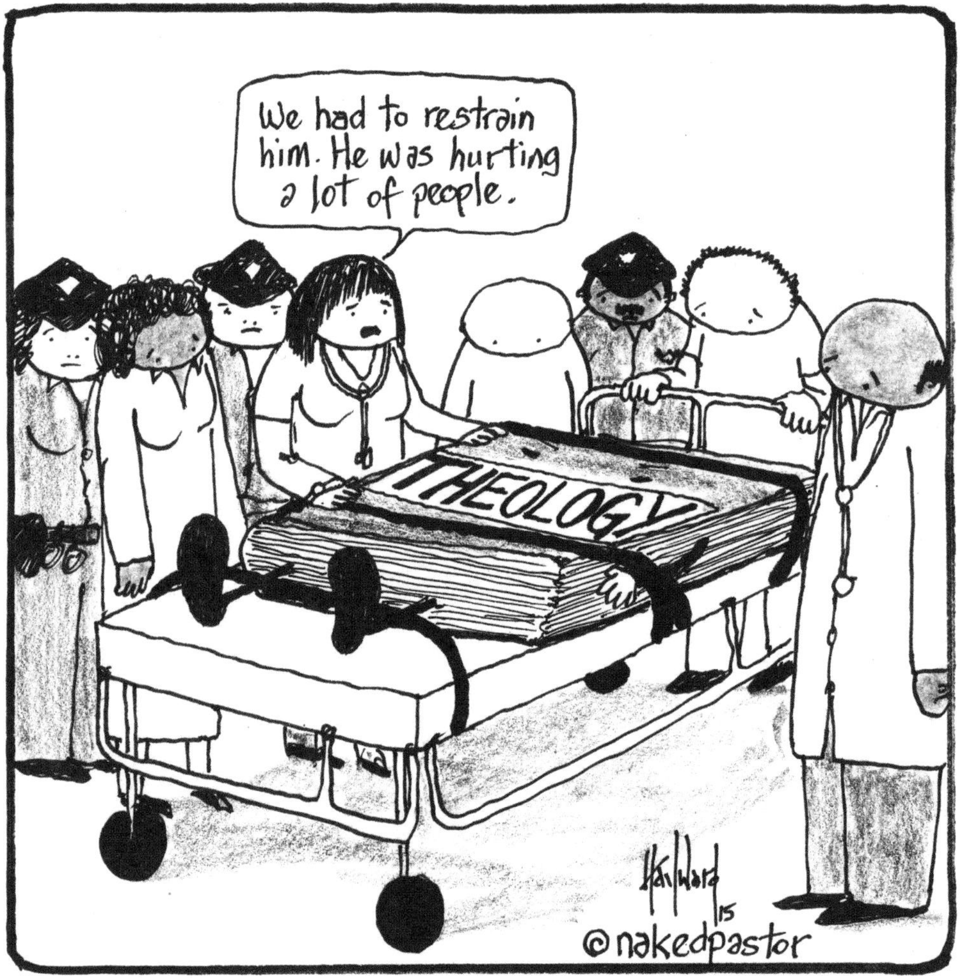
We had to restrain him. He was hurting a lot of people.
THEOLOGY
Hayward 15
@nakedpastor

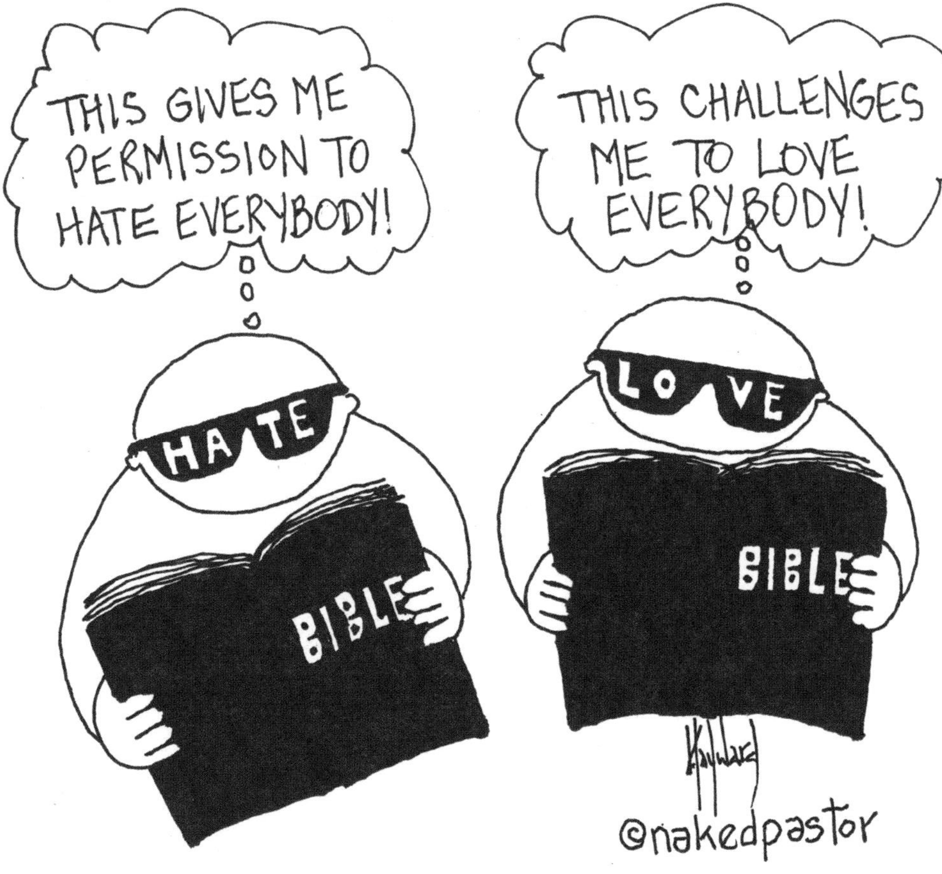
THIS GIVES ME PERMISSION TO HATE EVERYBODY!
HATE
BIBLE
THIS CHALLENGES ME TO LOVE EVERYBODY!
LOVE
BIBLE
@nakedpastor

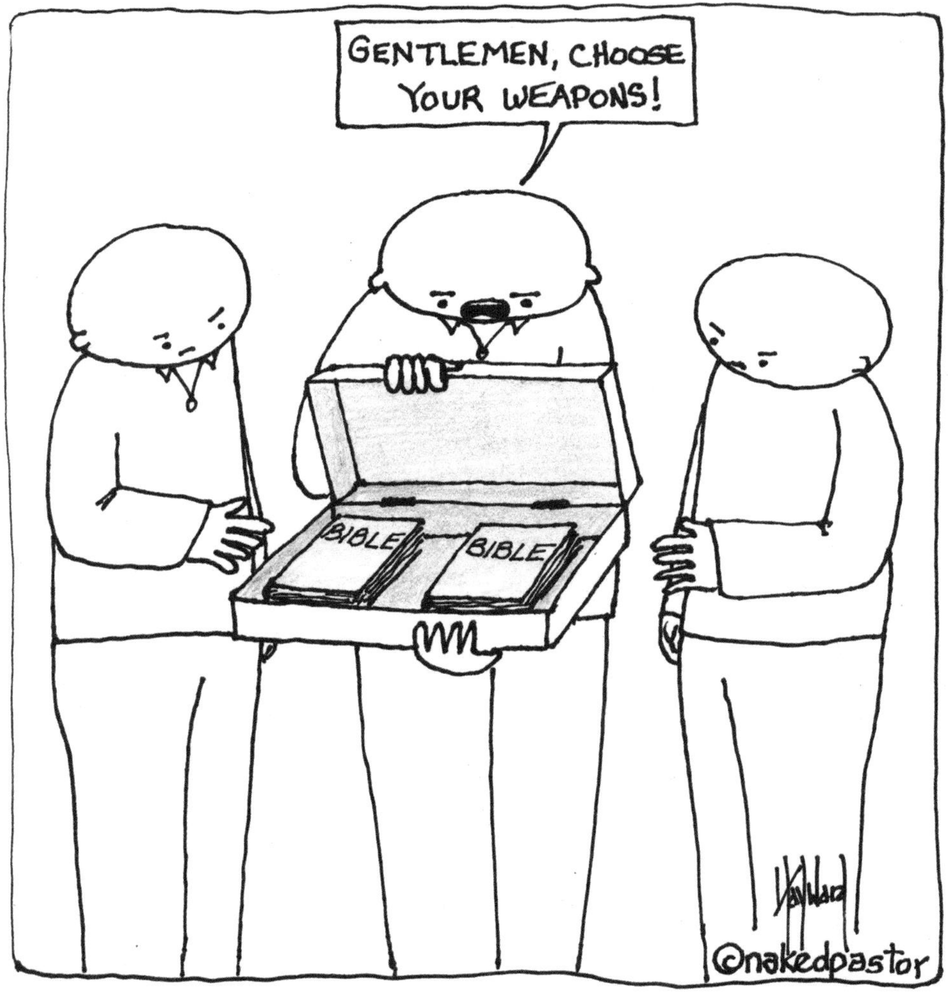
GENTLEMEN, CHOOSE YOUR WEAPONS!
BIBLE
BIBLE
©nakedpastor

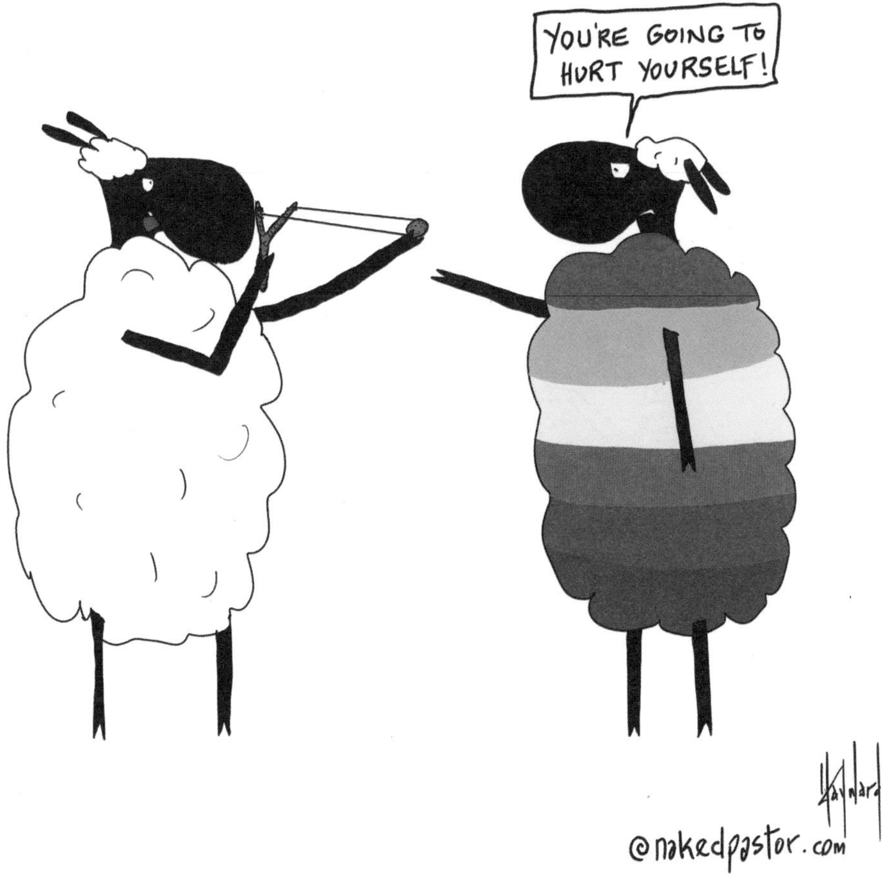
YOU'RE GOING TO HURT YOURSELF!
@nakedpastor.com

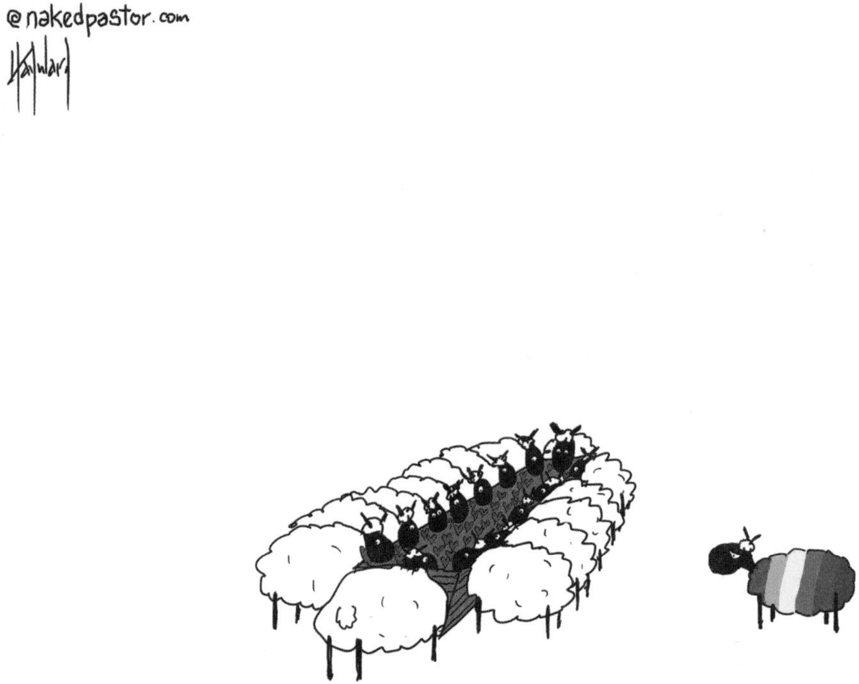
@nakedpastor.com
Hayward

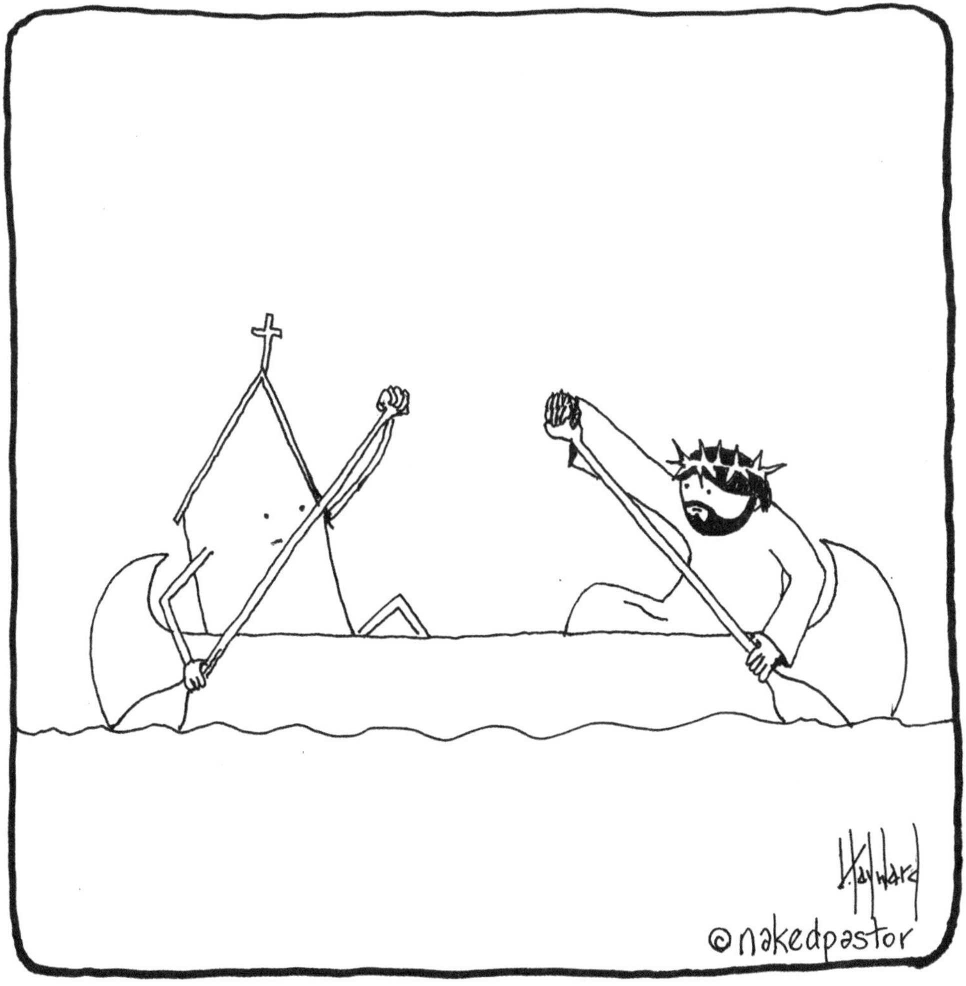
©nakedpastor

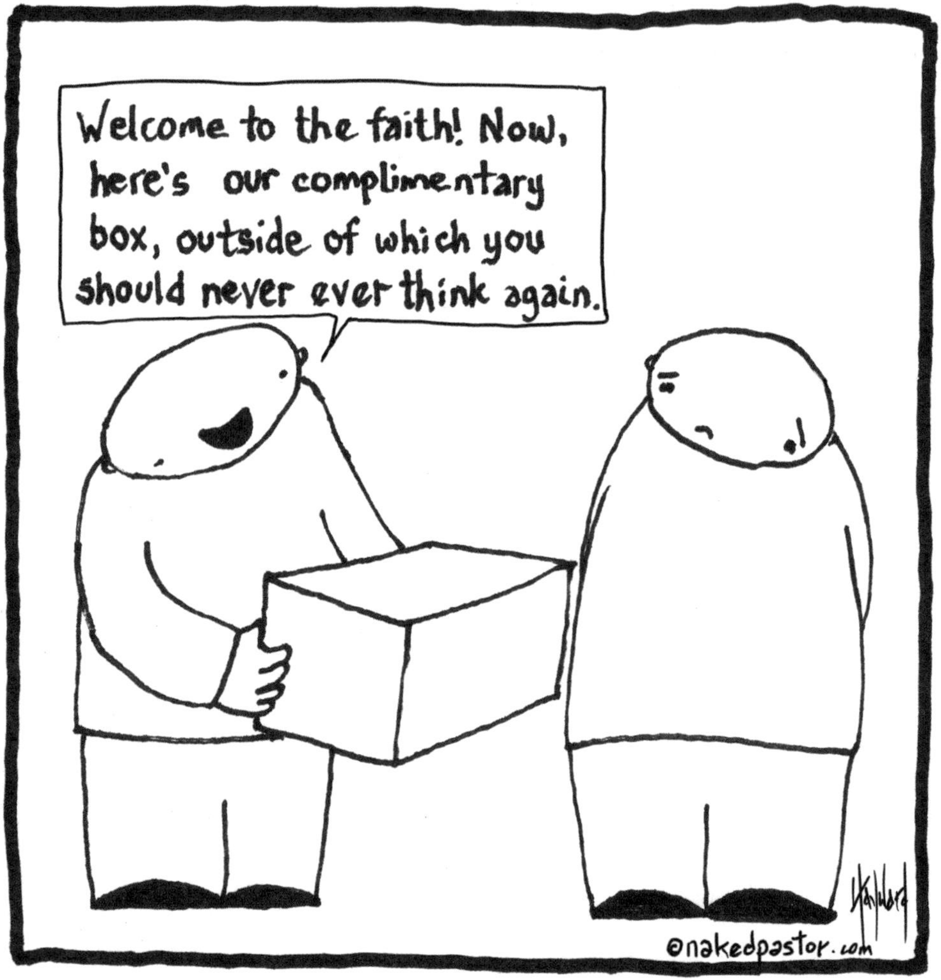
Welcome to the faith! Now, here's our complimentary box, outside of which you should never ever think again.
Hayward
©nakedpastor.com

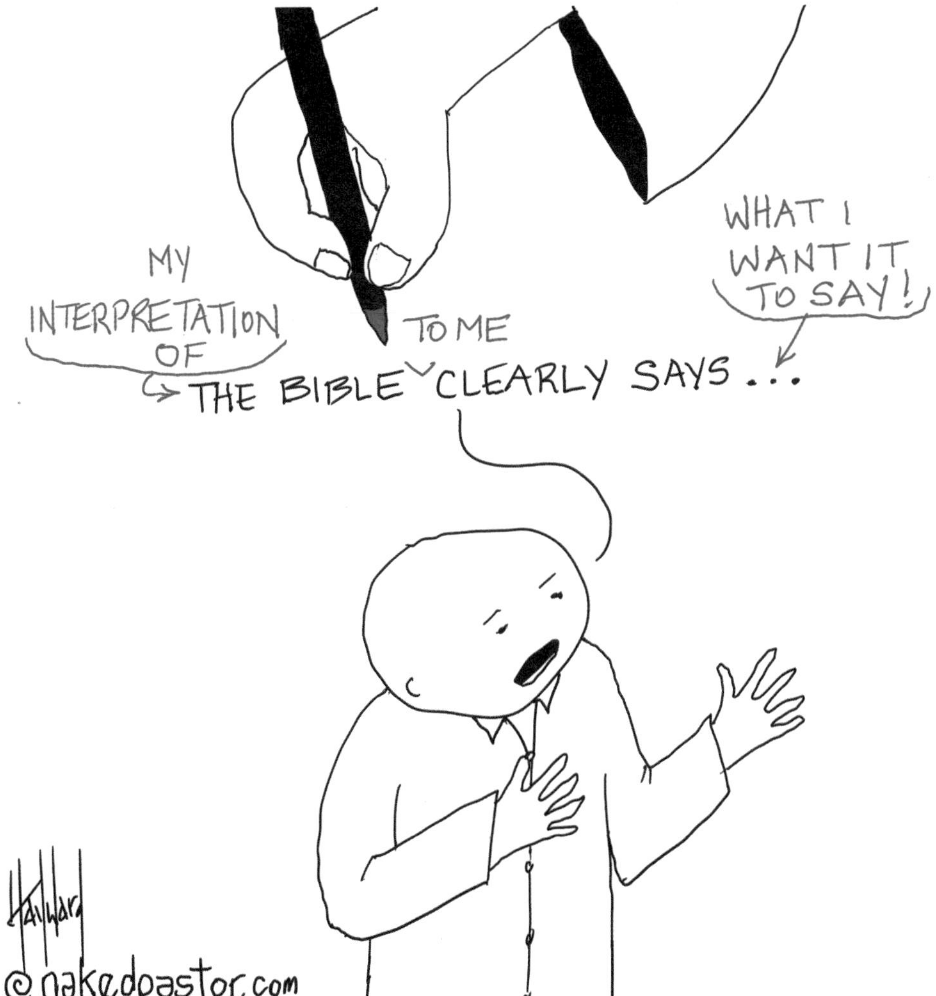
MY INTERPRETATION OF
TO ME
WHAT I WANT IT TO SAY!
THE BIBLE CLEARLY SAYS...
©nakedpastor.com

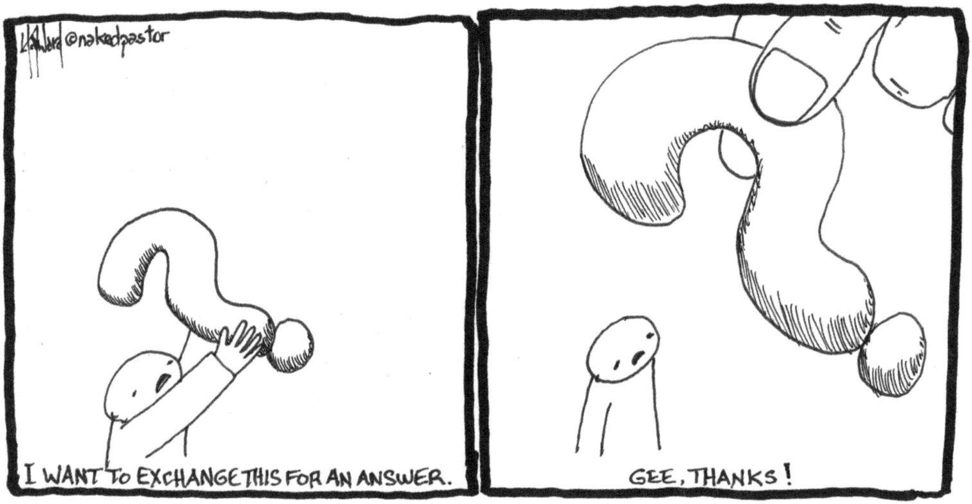
@nakedpastor
I WANT TO EXCHANGE THIS FOR AN ANSWER.
GEE, THANKS!

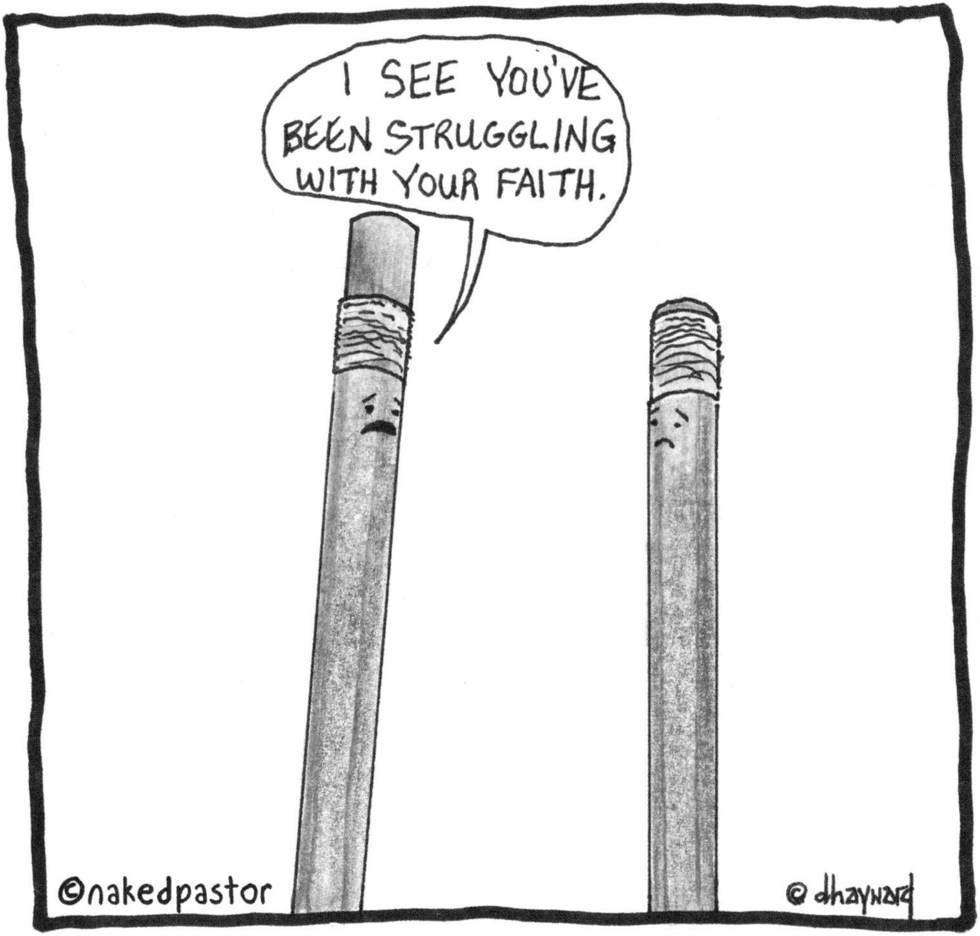
I SEE YOU'VE BEEN STRUGGLING WITH YOUR FAITH.
©nakedpastor
@dhayward

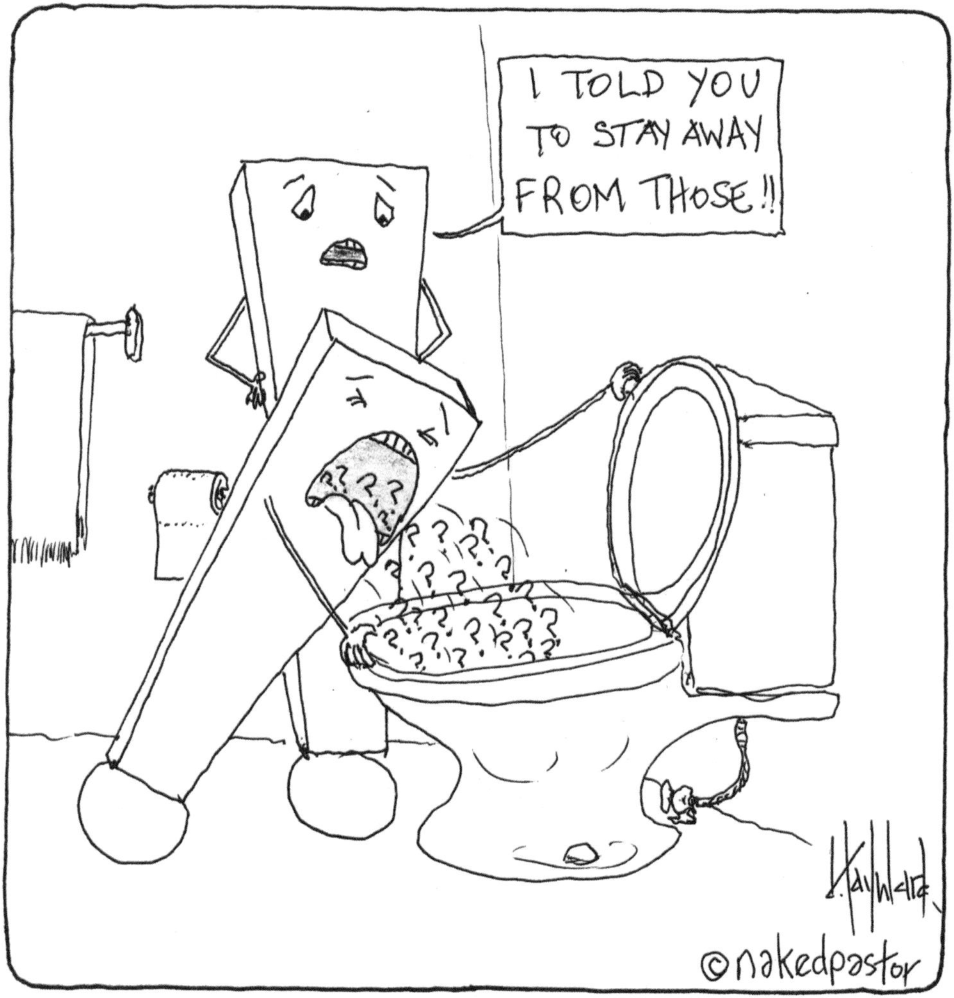
I TOLD YOU TO STAY AWAY FROM THOSE!!
Hayward
©nakedpastor

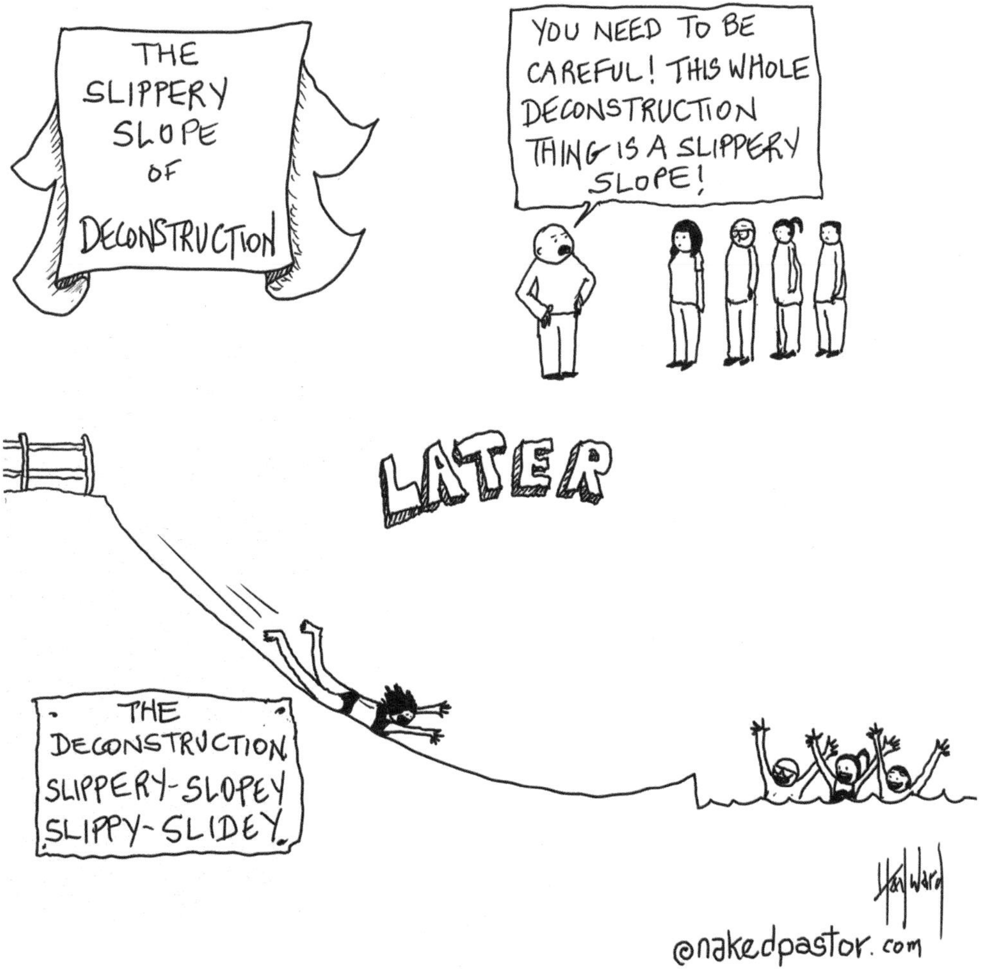
THE SLIPPERY SLOPE OF DECONSTRUCTION
YOU NEED TO BE CAREFUL! THIS WHOLE DECONSTRUCTION THING IS A SLIPPERY SLOPE!
LATER
THE DECONSTRUCTION SLIPPERY-SLOPEY SLIPPY-SLIDEY
Hayward
@nakedpastor.com

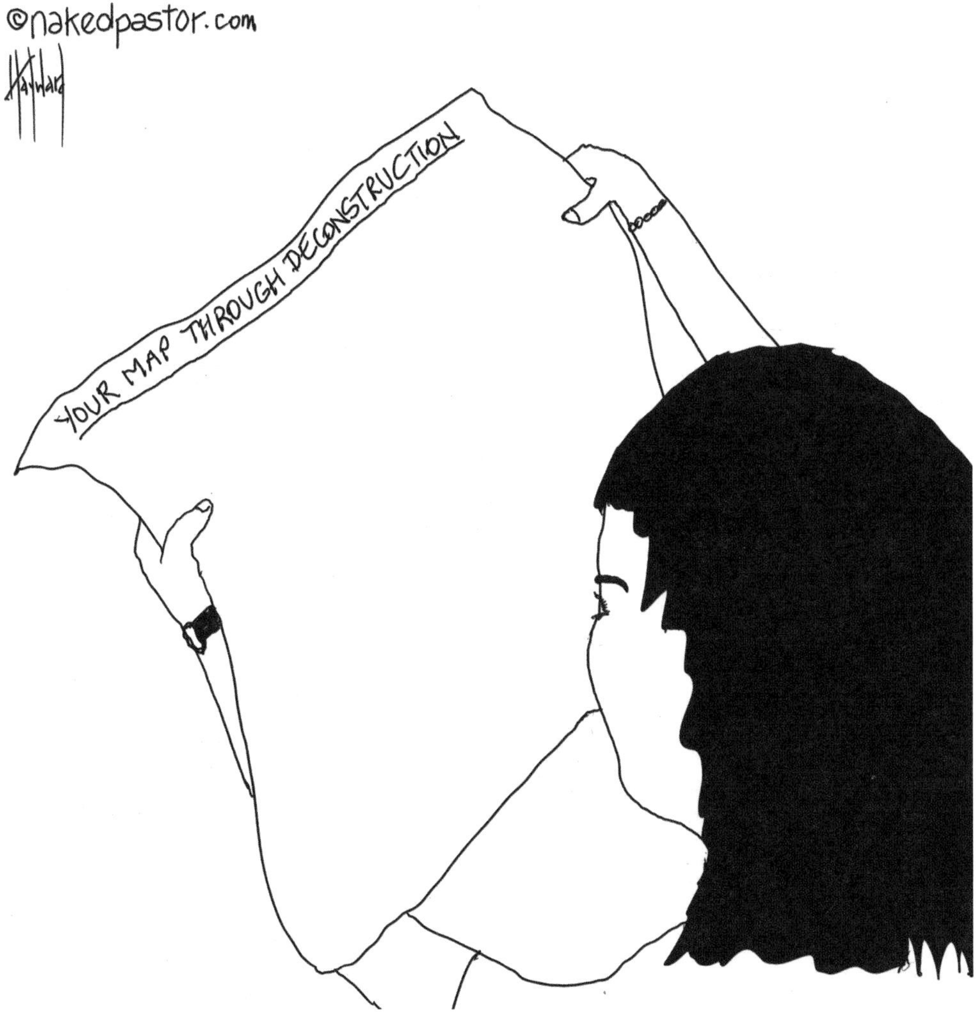
©nakedpastor.com
Hayward
YOUR MAP THROUGH DECONSTRUCTION

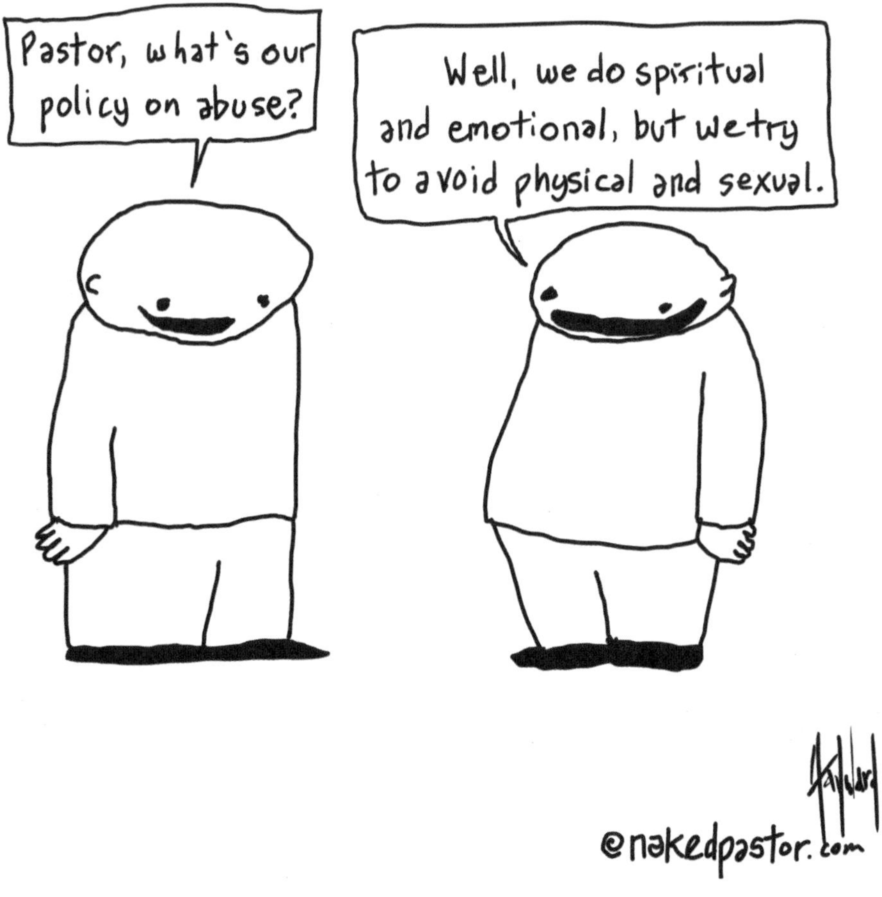
Pastor, what's our policy on abuse?
Well, we do spiritual and emotional, but we try to avoid physical and sexual.
©nakedpastor.com

Google Translate
Text
Documents
CHRISTIANESE-DETECTED
ENGLISH
We need to pray for Suzie.
Hey did you hear about Suzie?
©nakedpastor.com

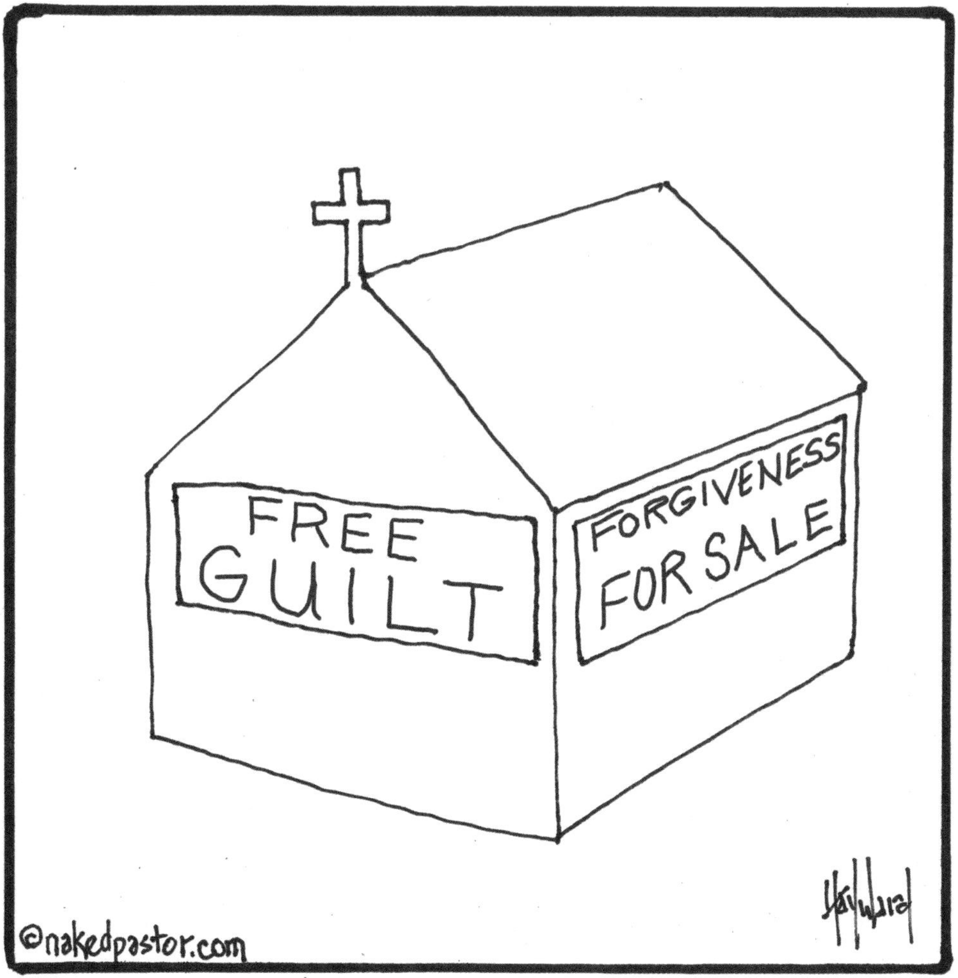
FREE
GUILT
FORGIVENESS
FOR SALE
©nakedpastor.com

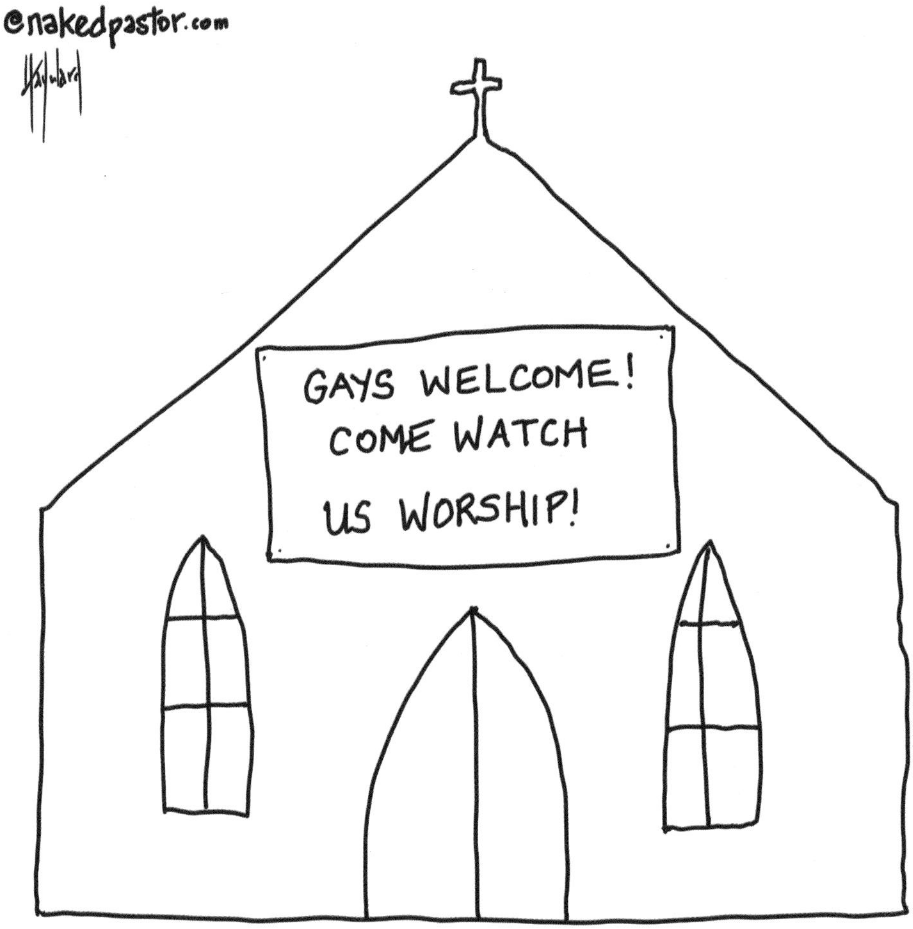
@nakedpastor.com
GAYS WELCOME! COME WATCH US WORSHIP!

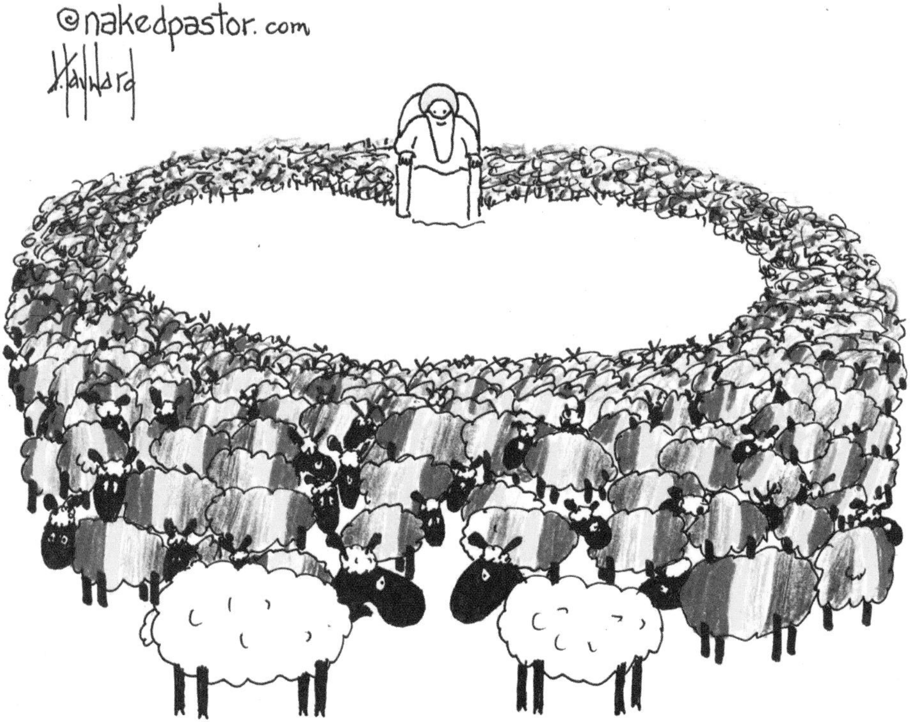
©nakedpastor.com
Hayward

"I KNOW THE BIBLE SAYS THERE'S A RAINBOW AROUND GOD'S THRONE, BUT THIS IS NOT WHAT I EXPECTED!"

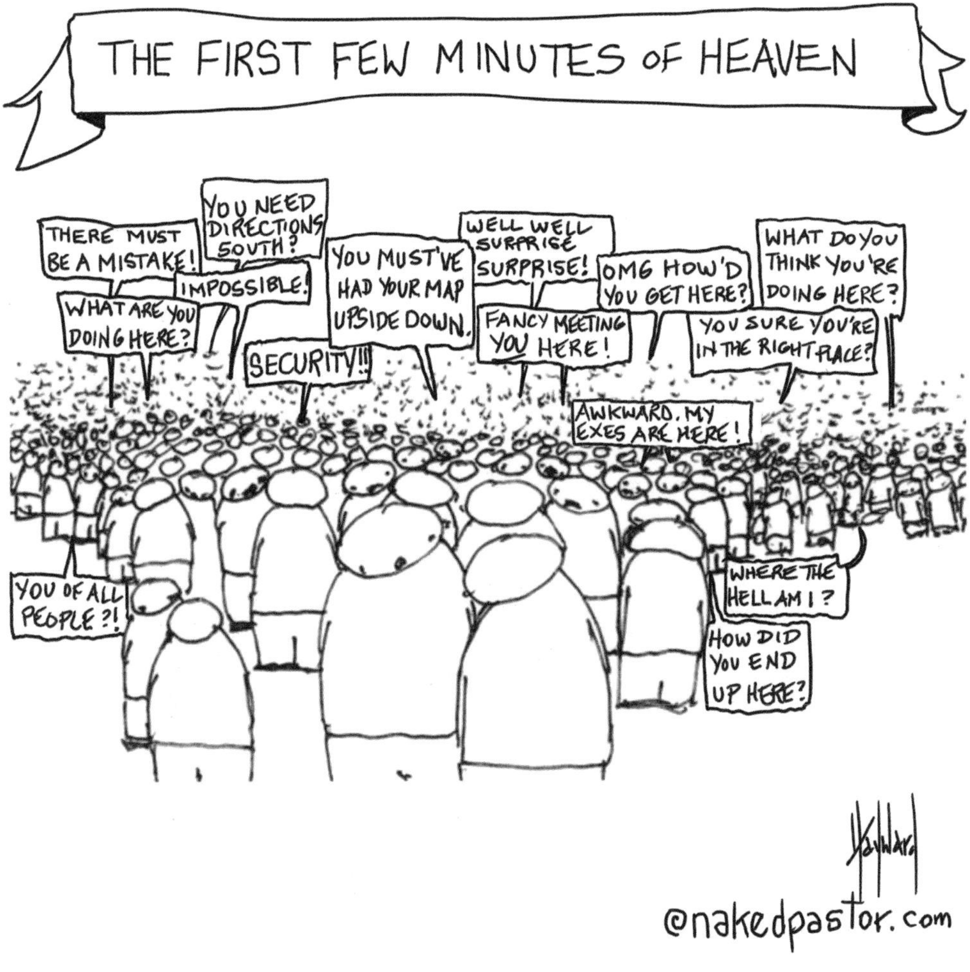
THE FIRST FEW MINUTES OF HEAVEN
THERE MUST BE A MISTAKE!
YOU NEED DIRECTIONS SOUTH?
IMPOSSIBLE!
WHAT ARE YOU DOING HERE?
SECURITY!!
YOU MUST'VE HAD YOUR MAP UPSIDE DOWN.
WELL WELL SURPRISE SURPRISE!
FANCY MEETING YOU HERE!
OMG HOW'D YOU GET HERE?
WHAT DO YOU THINK YOU'RE DOING HERE?
YOU SURE YOU'RE IN THE RIGHT PLACE?
AWKWARD. MY EXES ARE HERE!
YOU OF ALL PEOPLE?!
WHERE THE HELL AM I?
HOW DID YOU END UP HERE?
@nakedpastor.com

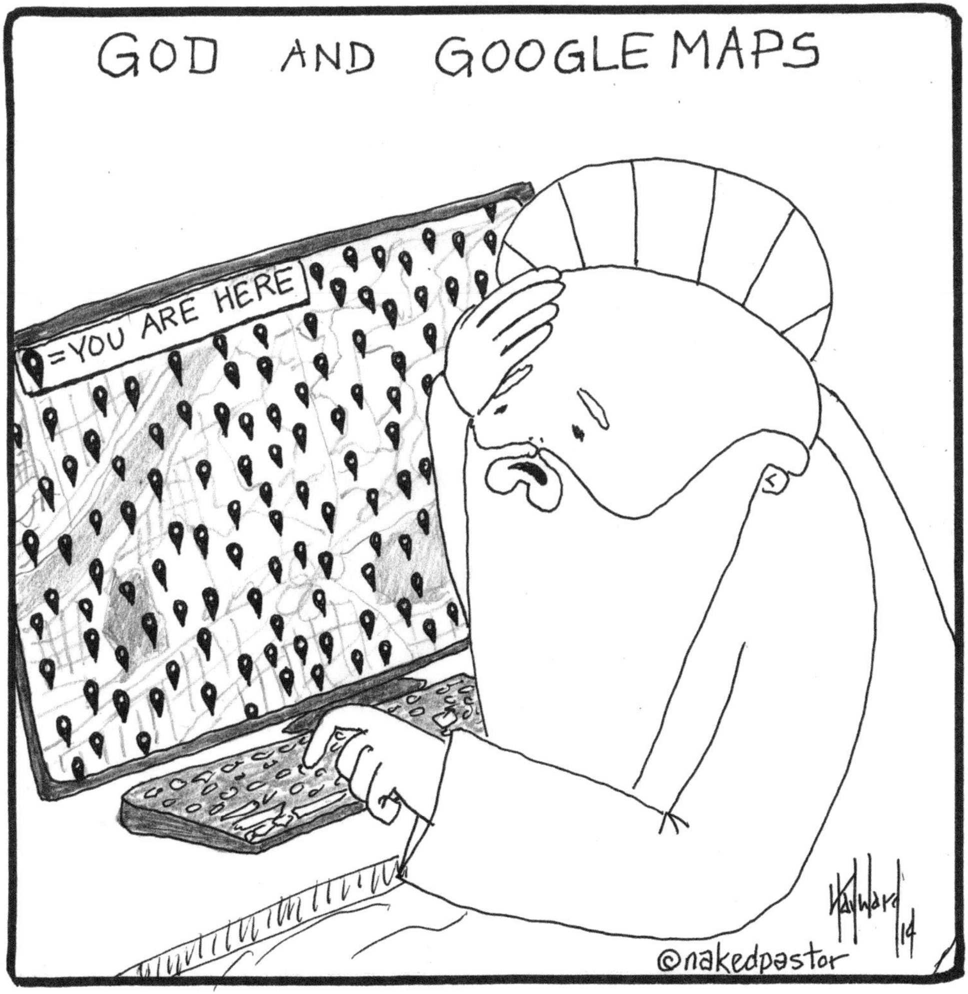
GOD AND GOOGLE MAPS
=YOU ARE HERE
Hayward 14
©nakedpastor

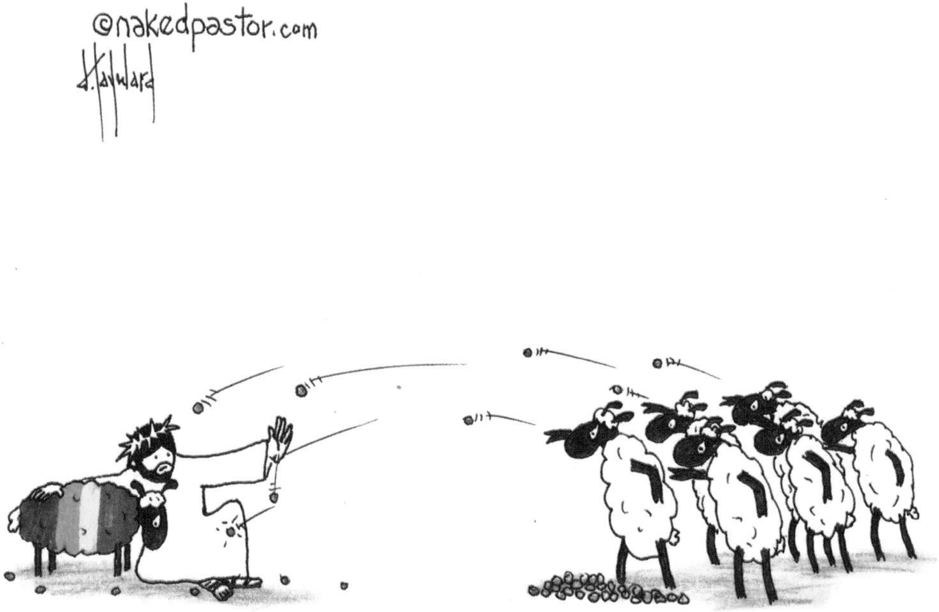
©nakedpastor.com
D. Hayward

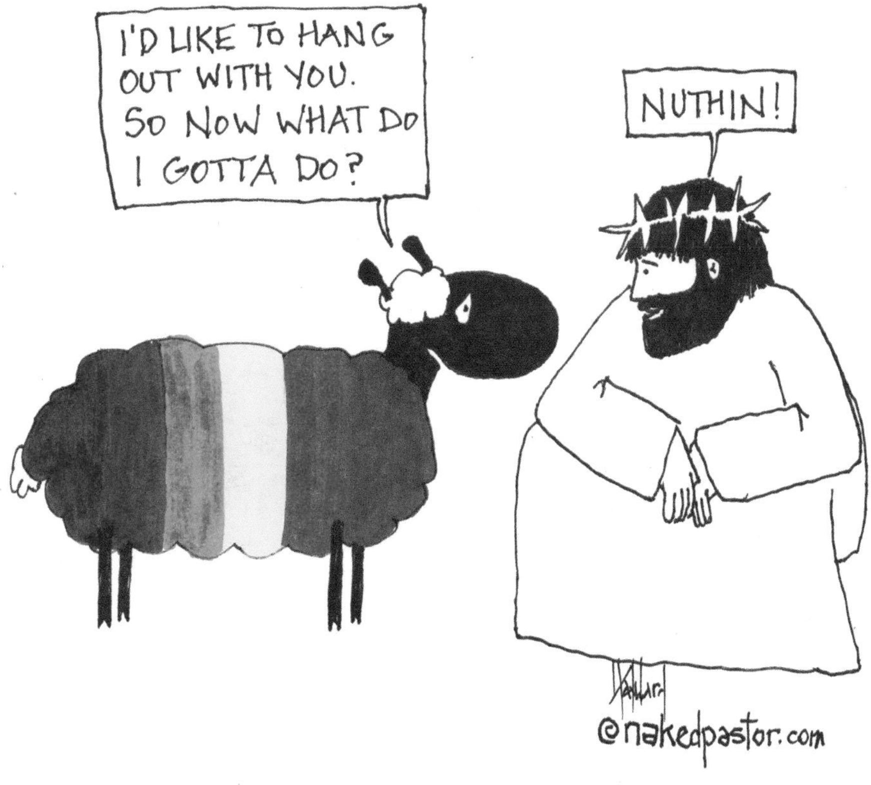
I'D LIKE TO HANG OUT WITH YOU. SO NOW WHAT DO I GOTTA DO?
NUTHIN!
©nakedpastor.com

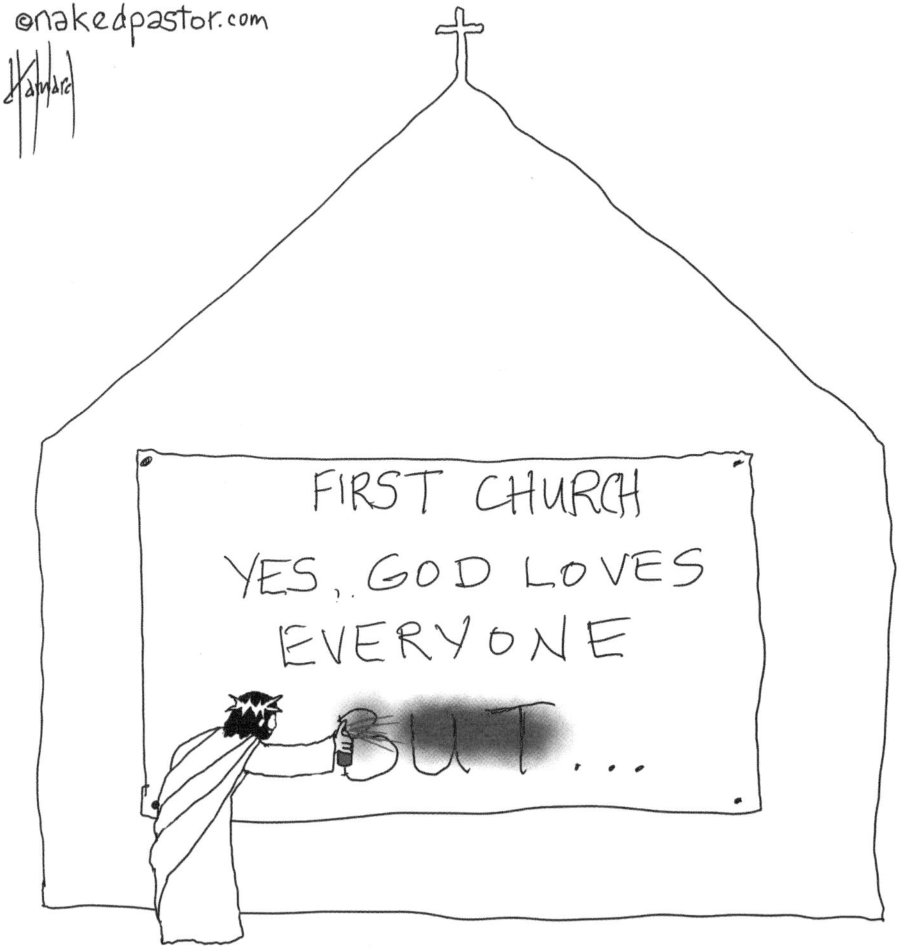
©nakedpastor.com
FIRST CHURCH
YES, GOD LOVES EVERYONE
BUT . . .

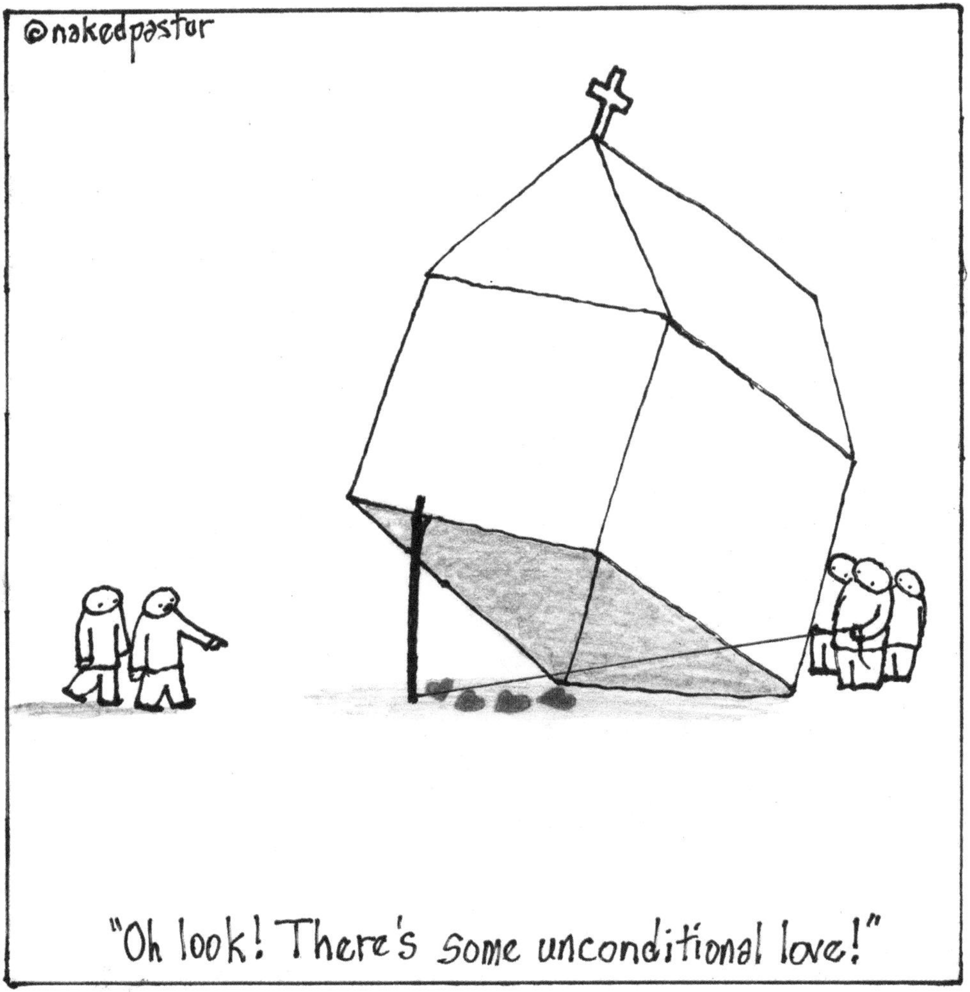
©nakedpastor
"Oh look! There's some unconditional love!"

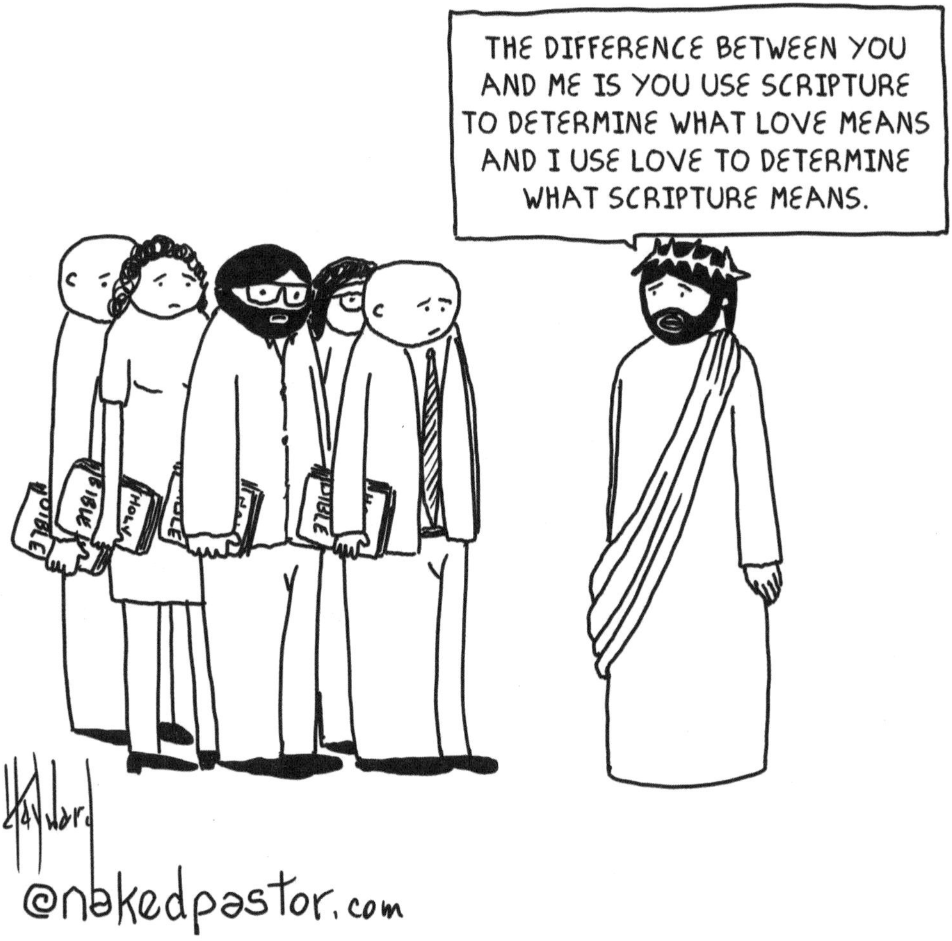
THE DIFFERENCE BETWEEN YOU AND ME IS YOU USE SCRIPTURE TO DETERMINE WHAT LOVE MEANS AND I USE LOVE TO DETERMINE WHAT SCRIPTURE MEANS.
BIBLE
HOLY BIBLE
BIBLE
BIBLE
Hayward
@nakedpastor.com

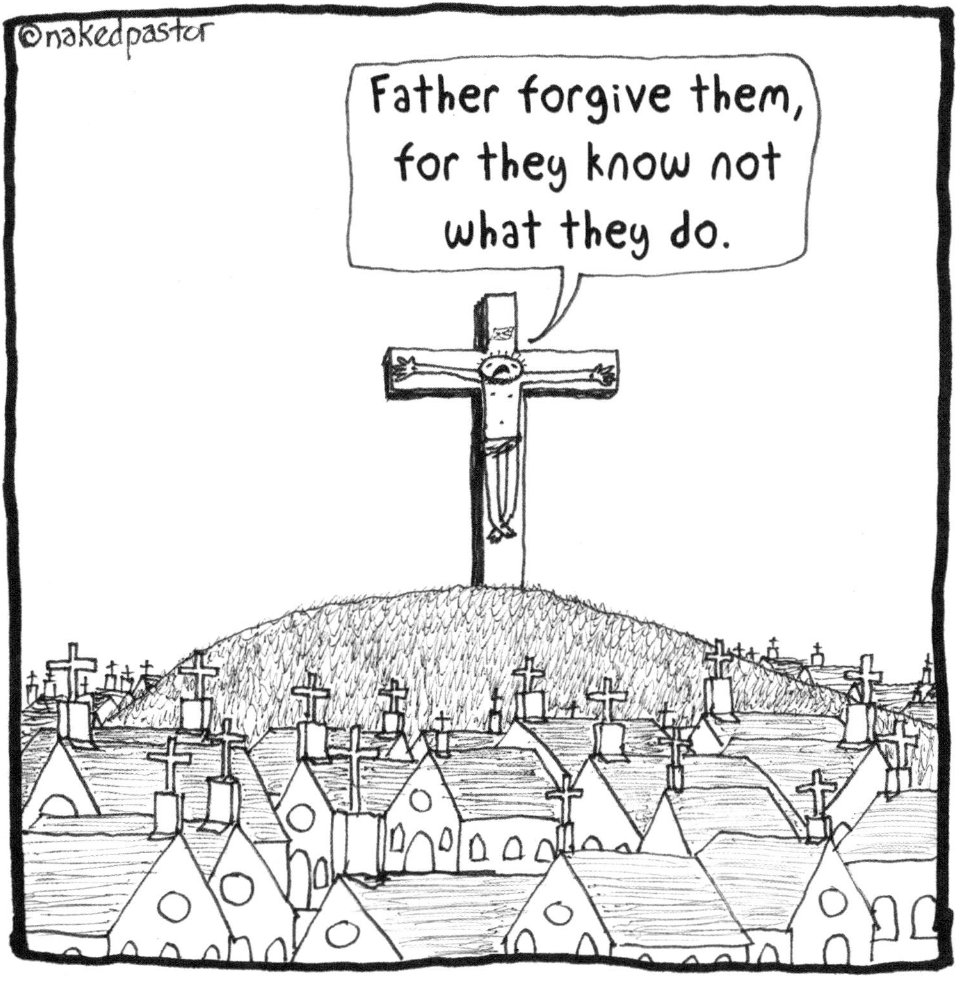
©nakedpastor
Father forgive them, for they know not what they do.

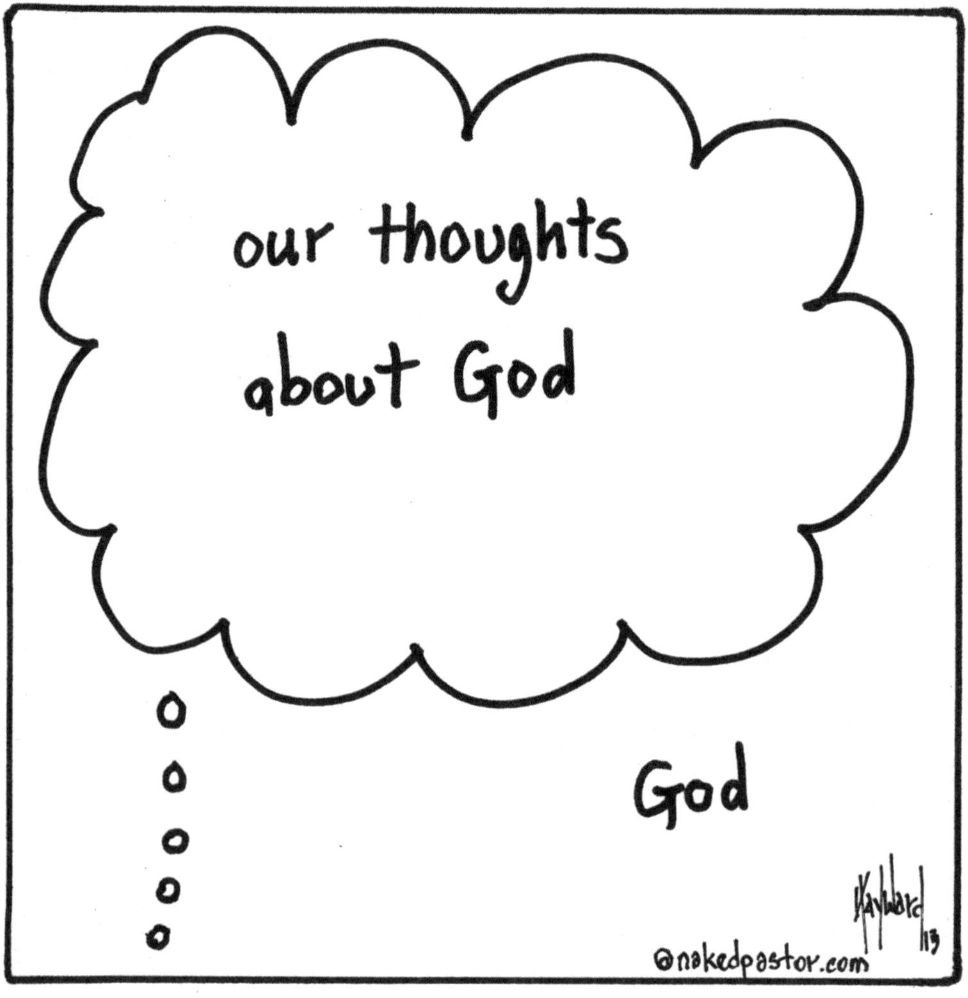
our thoughts about God
God
@nakedpastor.com
Hayward 13

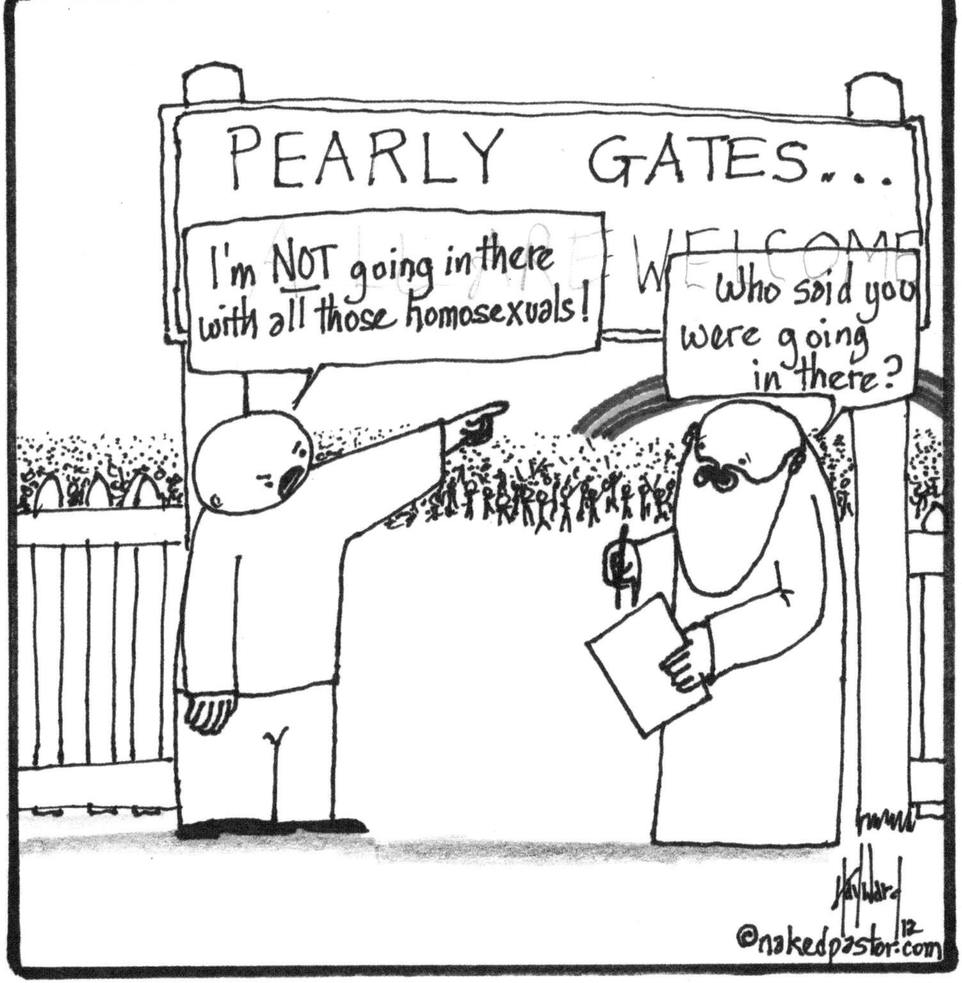
PEARLY GATES....
I'm NOT going in there with all those homosexuals!
Who said you were going in there?
©nakedpastor.com

© nakedpastor.com
Hayward
HOW HOLY YOU THINK YOU ARE
HOW MUCH OF A DICK YOU ARE

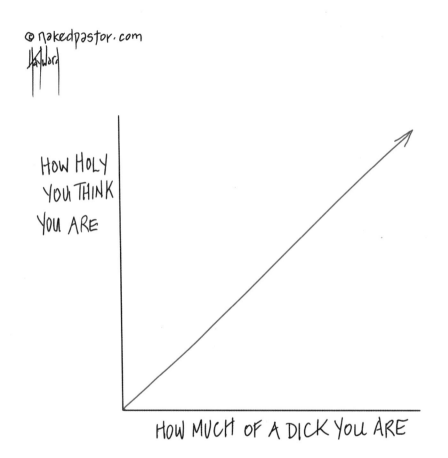

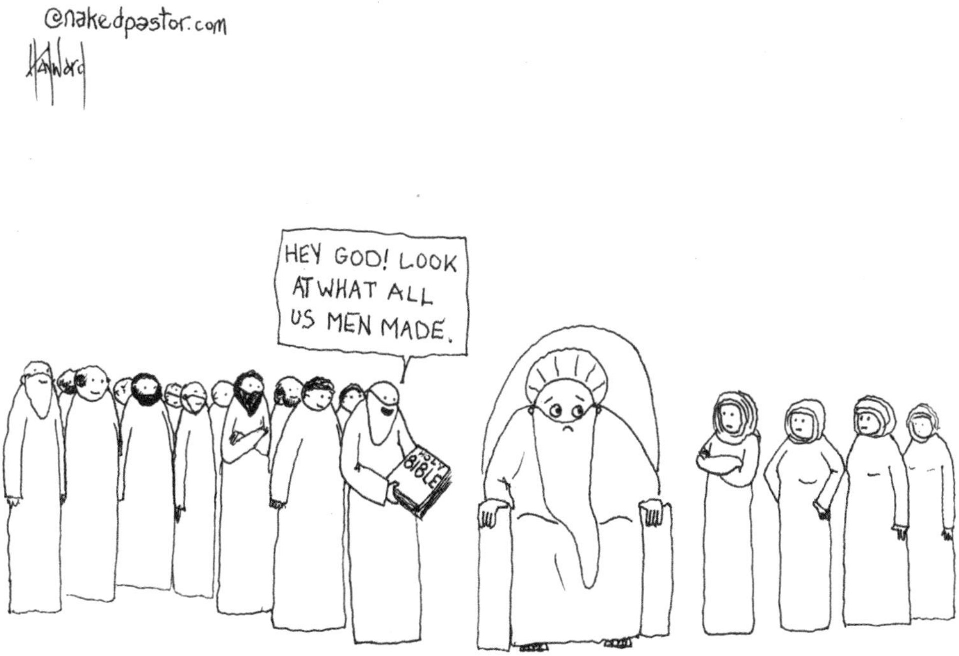

@nakedpastor.com
Hayward
HEY GOD! LOOK AT WHAT ALL US MEN MADE.
HOLY BIBLE

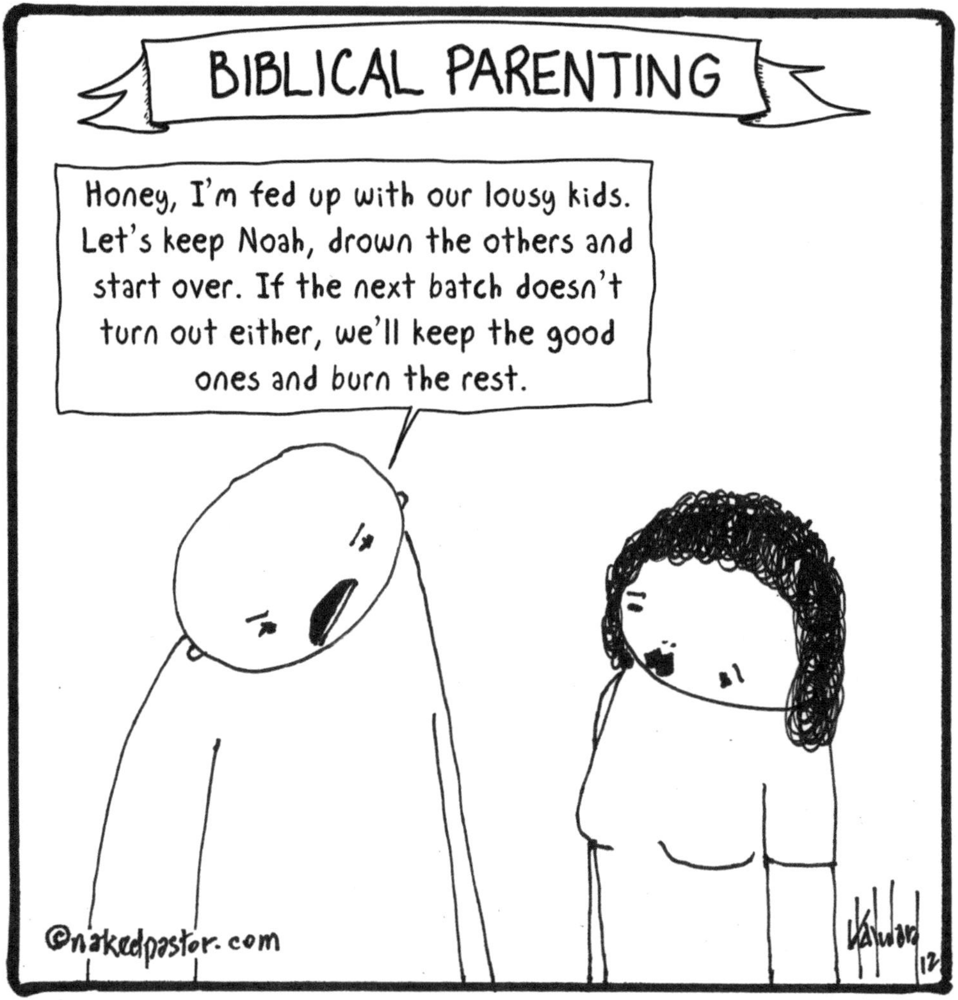
BIBLICAL PARENTING
Honey, I'm fed up with our lousy kids. Let's keep Noah, drown the others and start over. If the next batch doesn't turn out either, we'll keep the good ones and burn the rest.
©nakedpastor.com

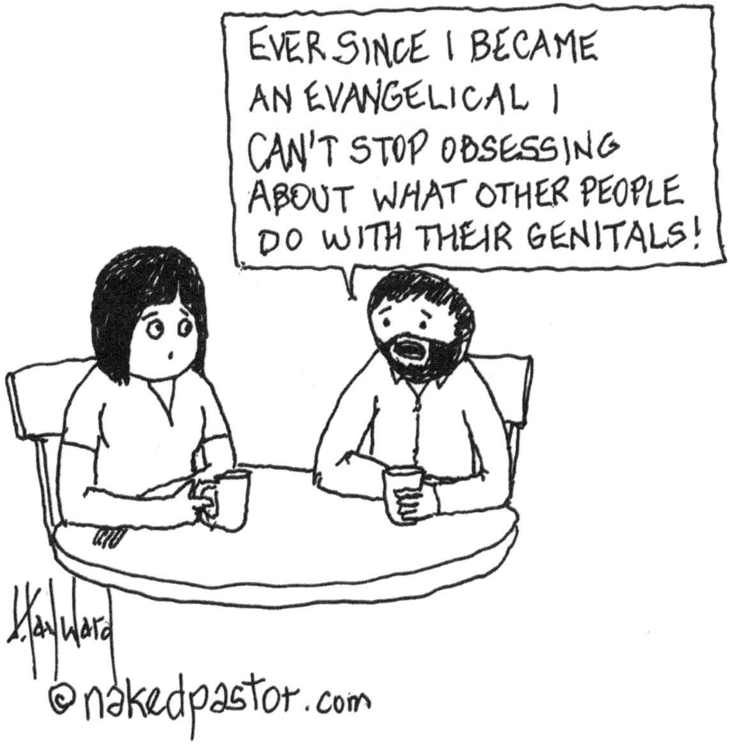
EVER SINCE I BECAME AN EVANGELICAL I CAN'T STOP OBSESSING ABOUT WHAT OTHER PEOPLE DO WITH THEIR GENITALS!
©nakedpastor.com

THE CHURCH & JESUS OVER THE YEARS

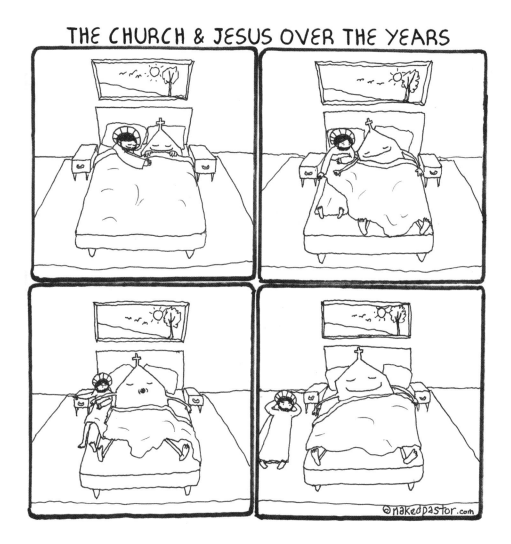

@nakedpastor.com

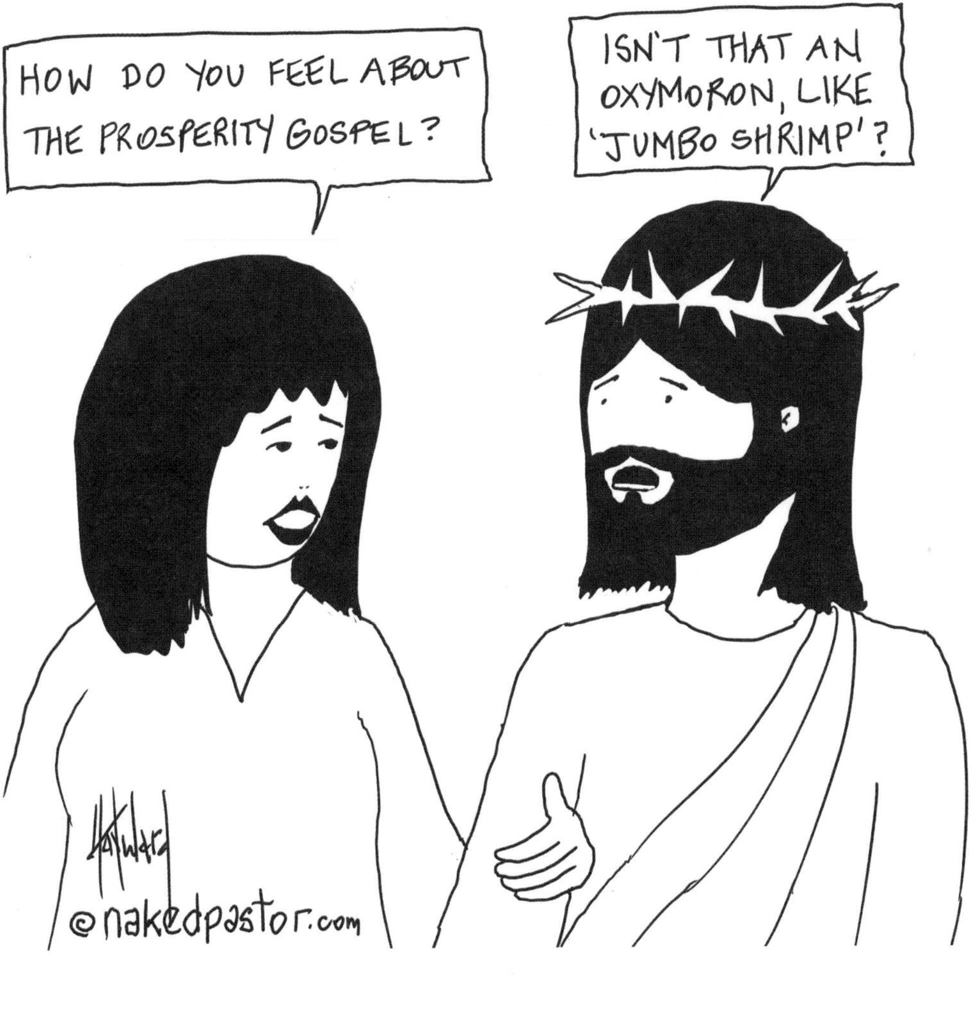
HOW DO YOU FEEL ABOUT THE PROSPERITY GOSPEL?
ISN'T THAT AN OXYMORON, LIKE 'JUMBO SHRIMP'?
Hayward
©nakedpastor.com

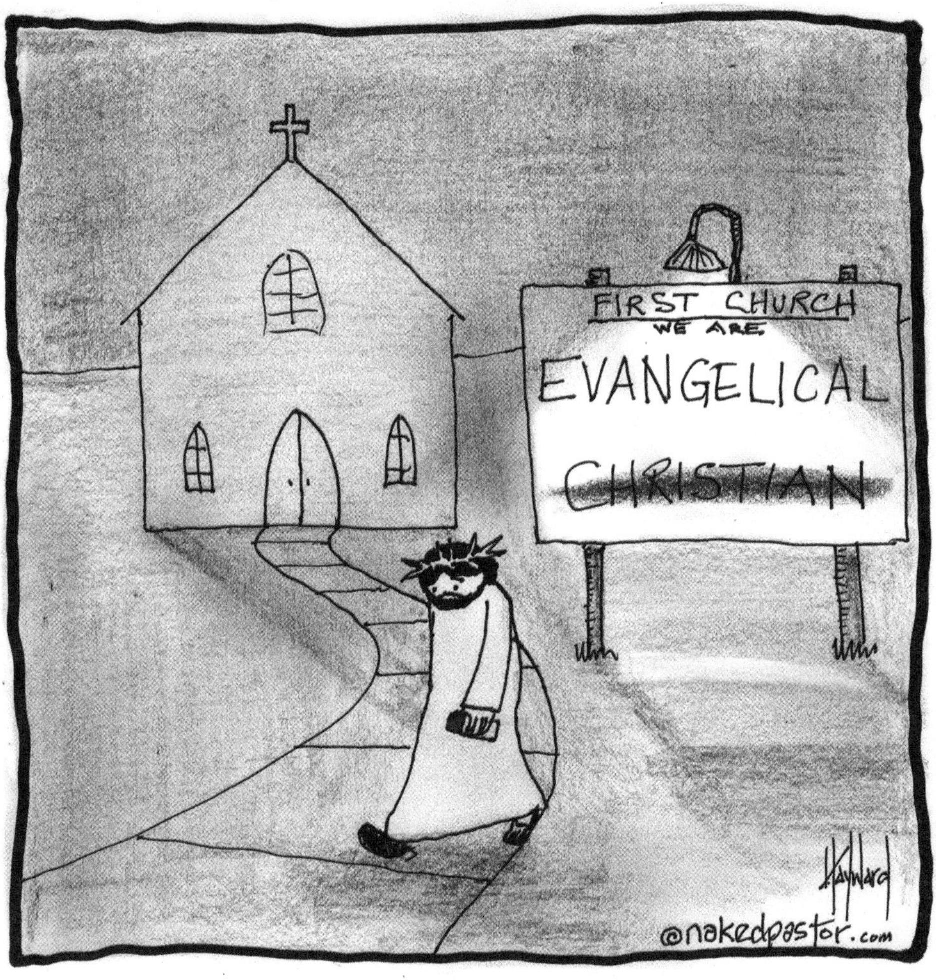
FIRST CHURCH
WE ARE
EVANGELICAL
CHRISTIAN
Hayward
@nakedpastor.com

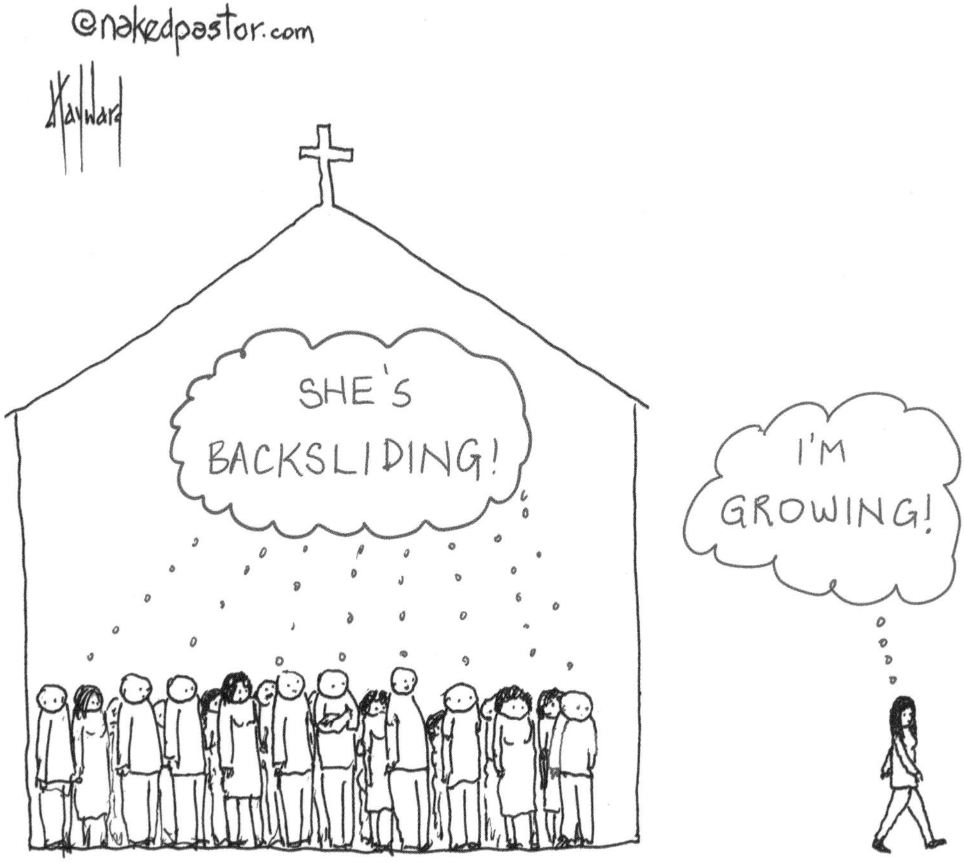
@nakedpastor.com
Hayward
SHE'S BACKSLIDING!
I'M GROWING!

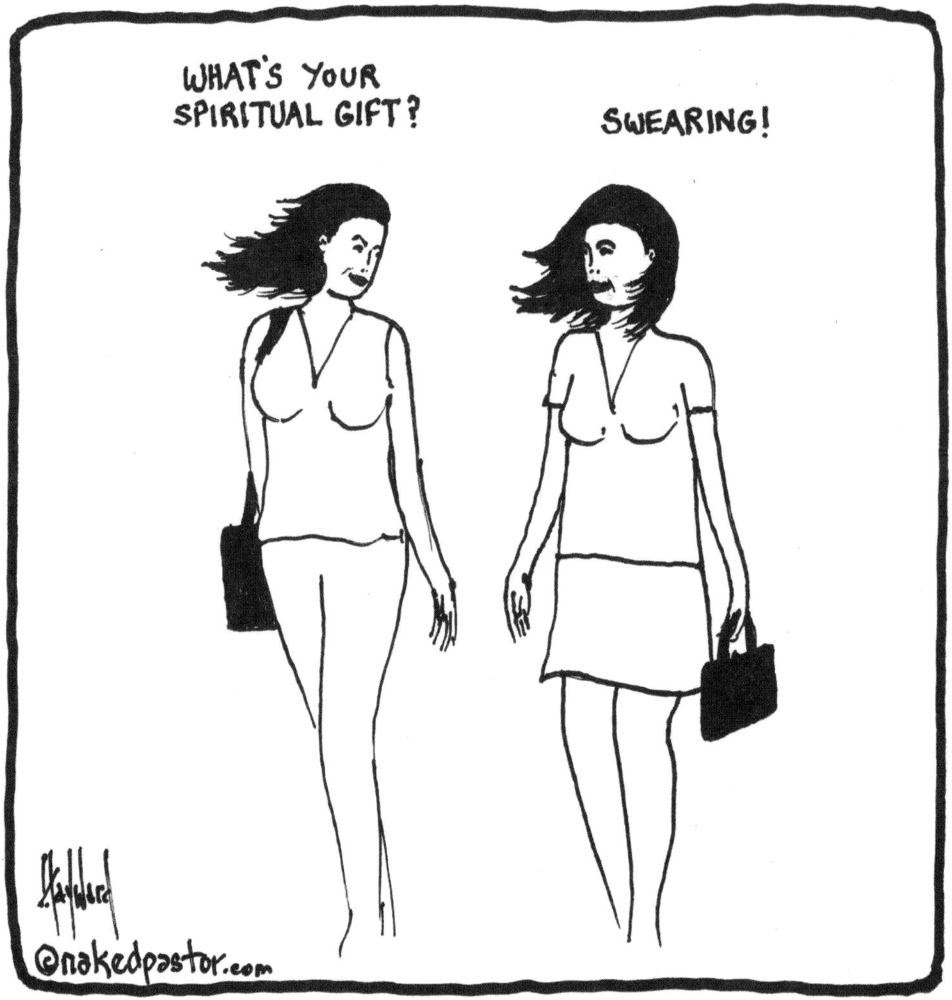
WHAT'S YOUR SPIRITUAL GIFT?
SWEARING!
©nakedpastor.com

"AND NOW YOU JUST FLIP IT LIKE THIS!"

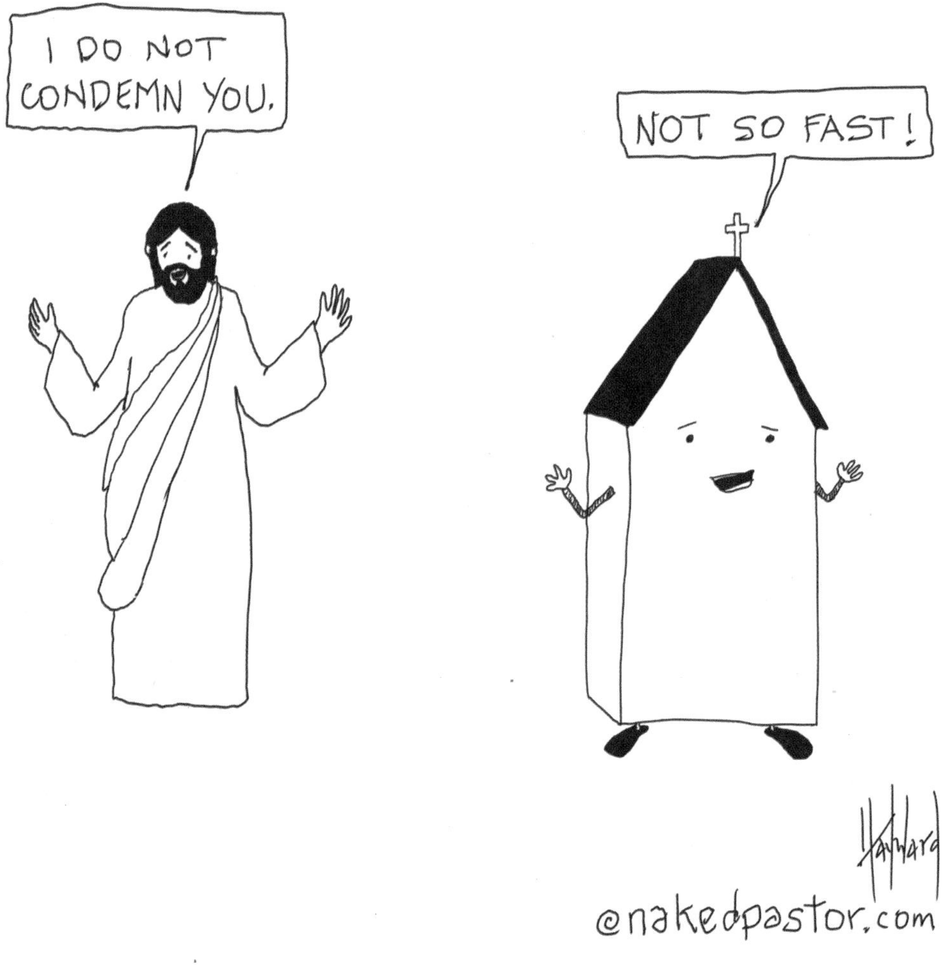
I DO NOT CONDEMN YOU.
NOT SO FAST!
Hayward
@nakedpastor.com

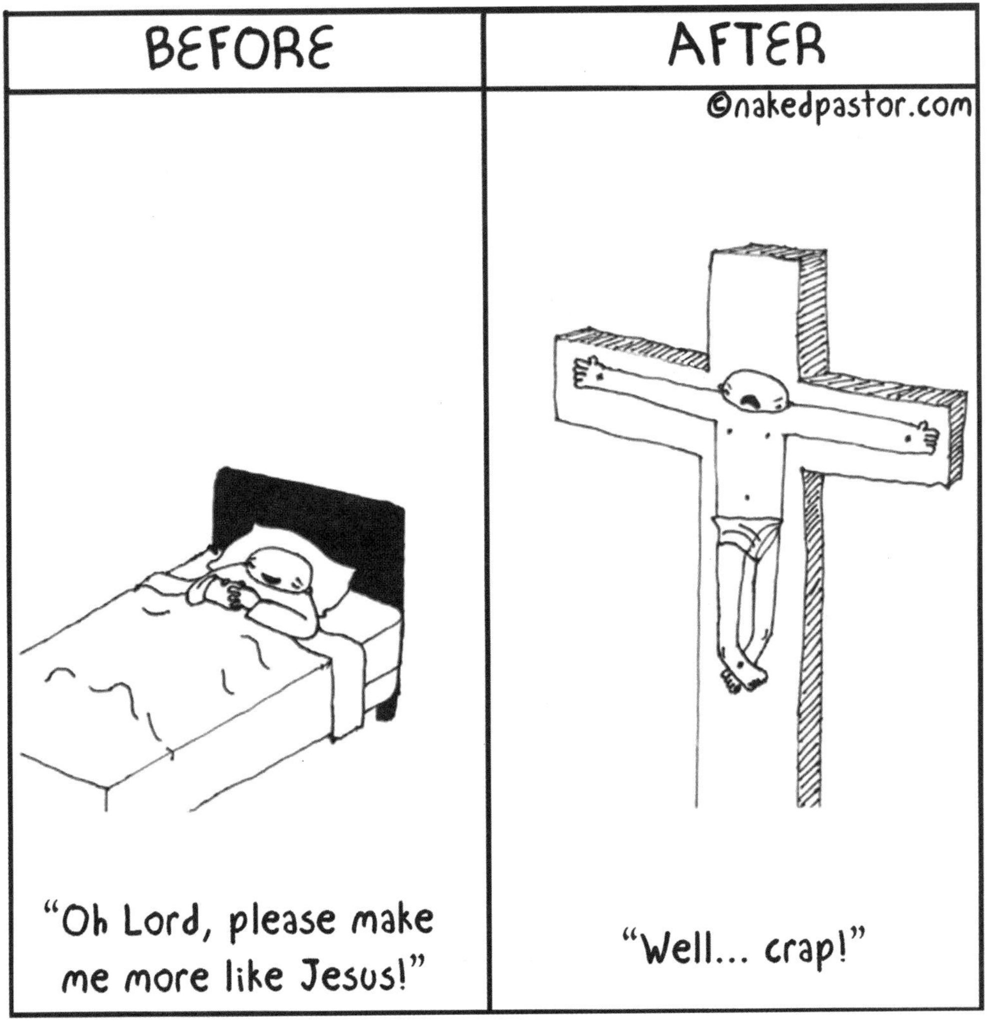
BEFORE
AFTER
©nakedpastor.com
"Oh Lord, please make me more like Jesus!"
"Well... crap!"

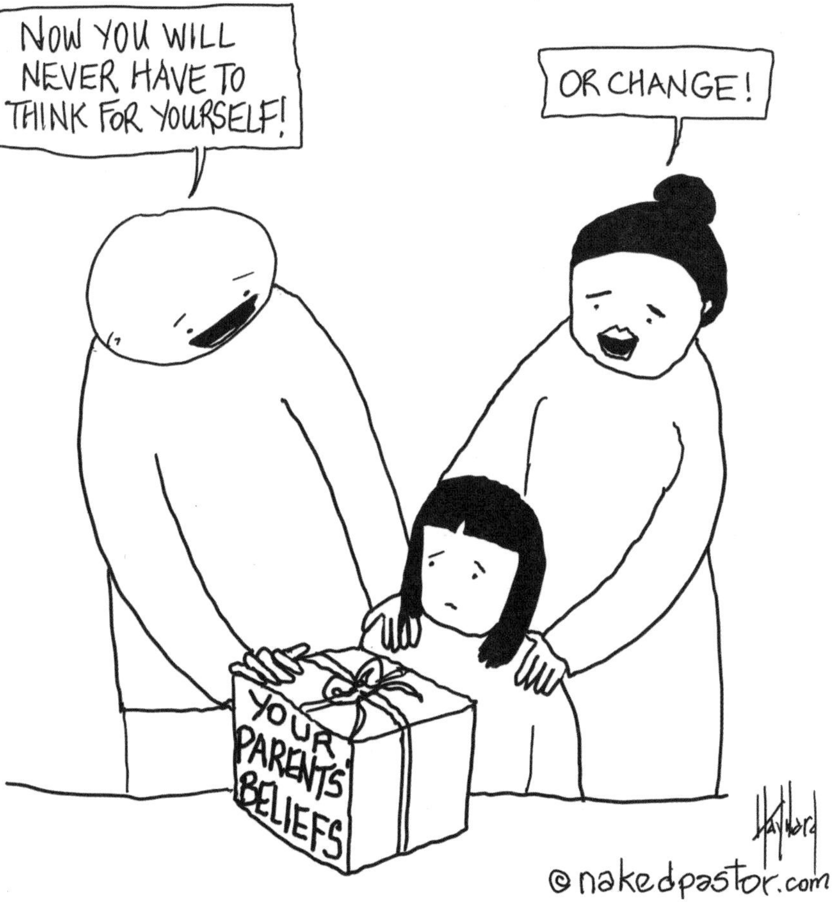
NOW YOU WILL NEVER HAVE TO THINK FOR YOURSELF!
OR CHANGE!
YOUR PARENTS' BELIEFS
Hayward
© nakedpastor.com

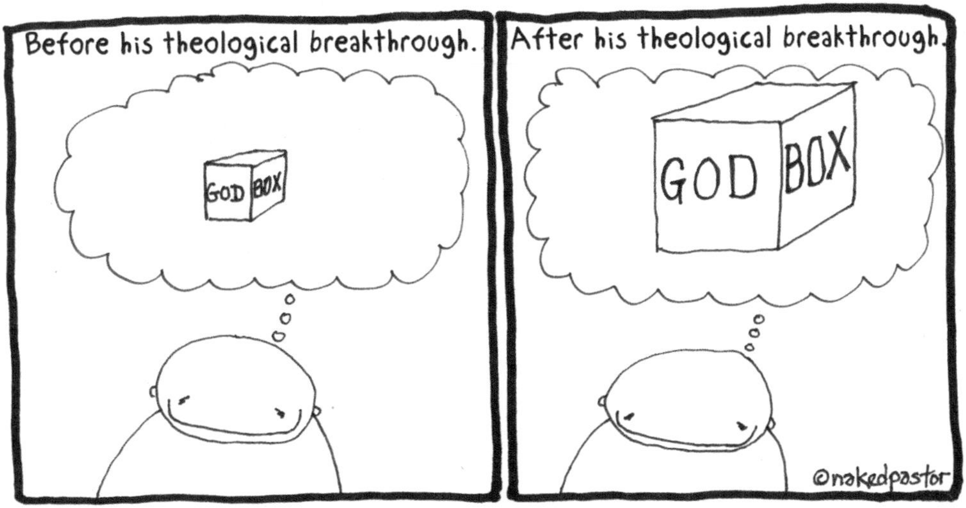
Before his theological breakthrough.
GOD BOX
After his theological breakthrough.
GOD BOX
©nakedpastor

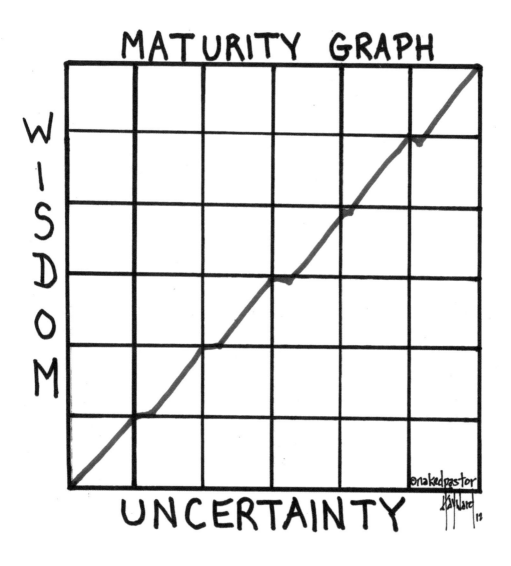

MATURITY GRAPH

WISDOM

UNCERTAINTY

@nakedpastor

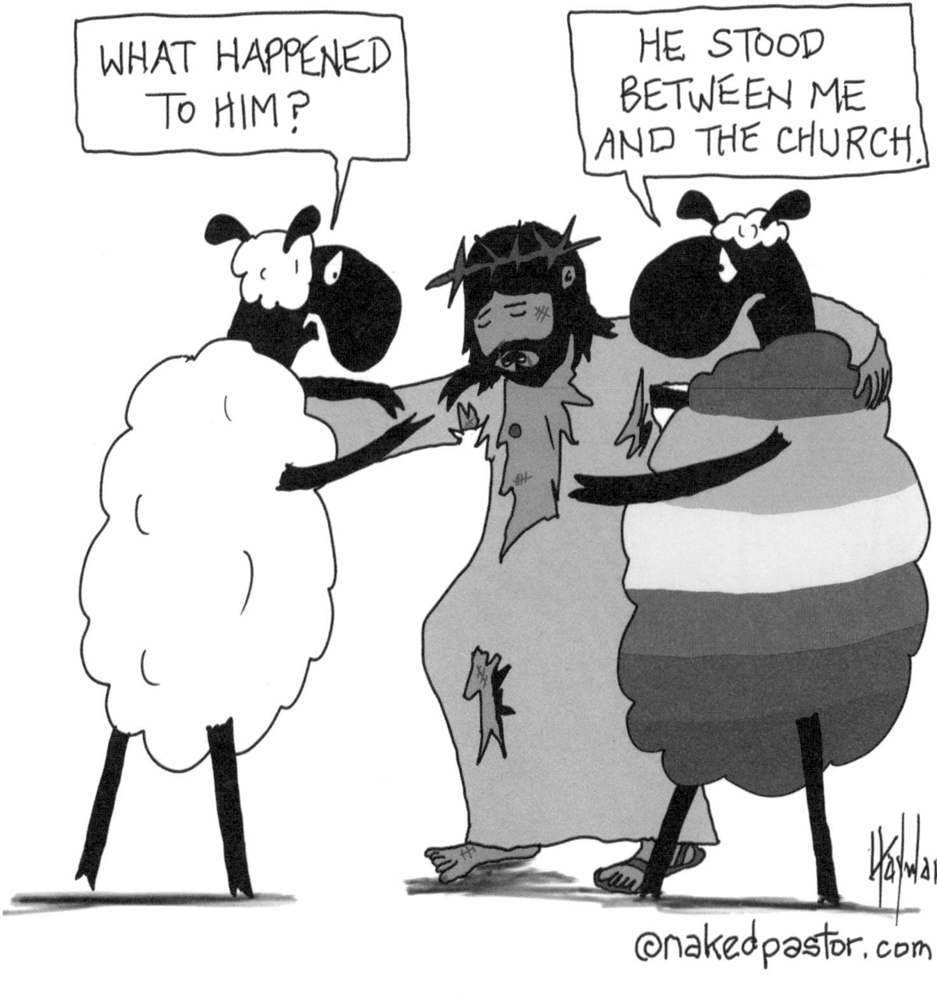
WHAT HAPPENED TO HIM?
HE STOOD BETWEEN ME AND THE CHURCH.
Hayward
©nakedpastor.com

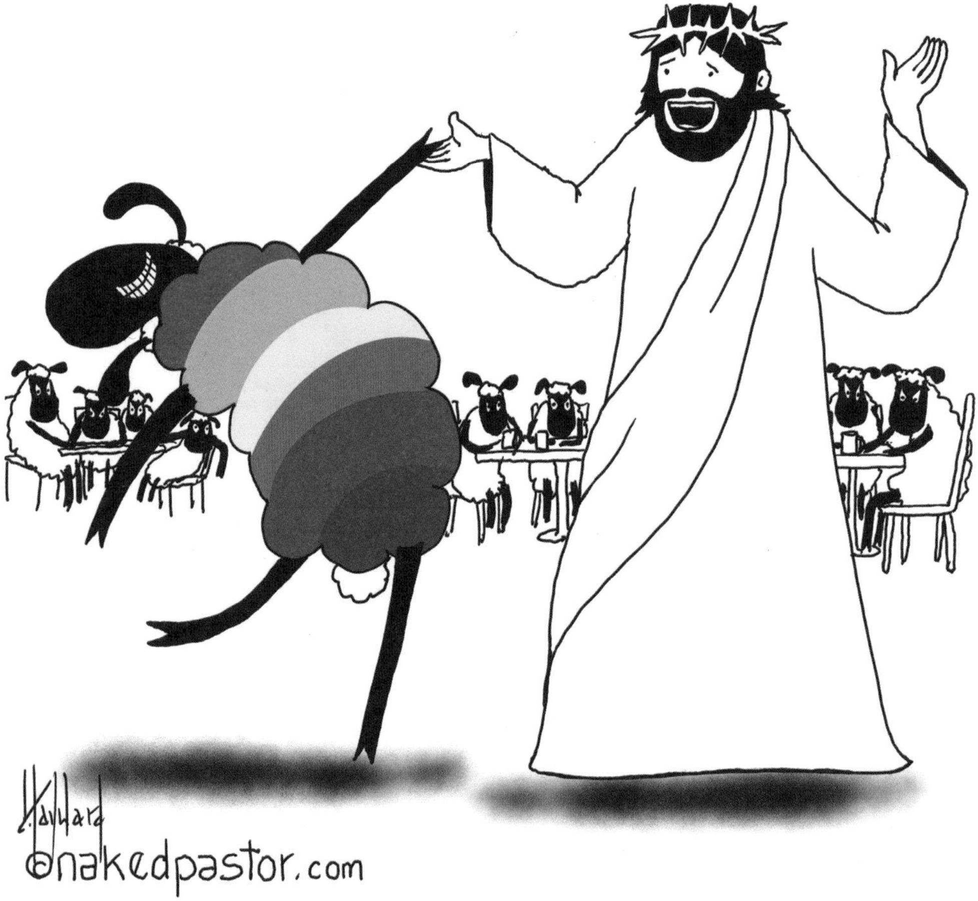
@nakedpastor.com

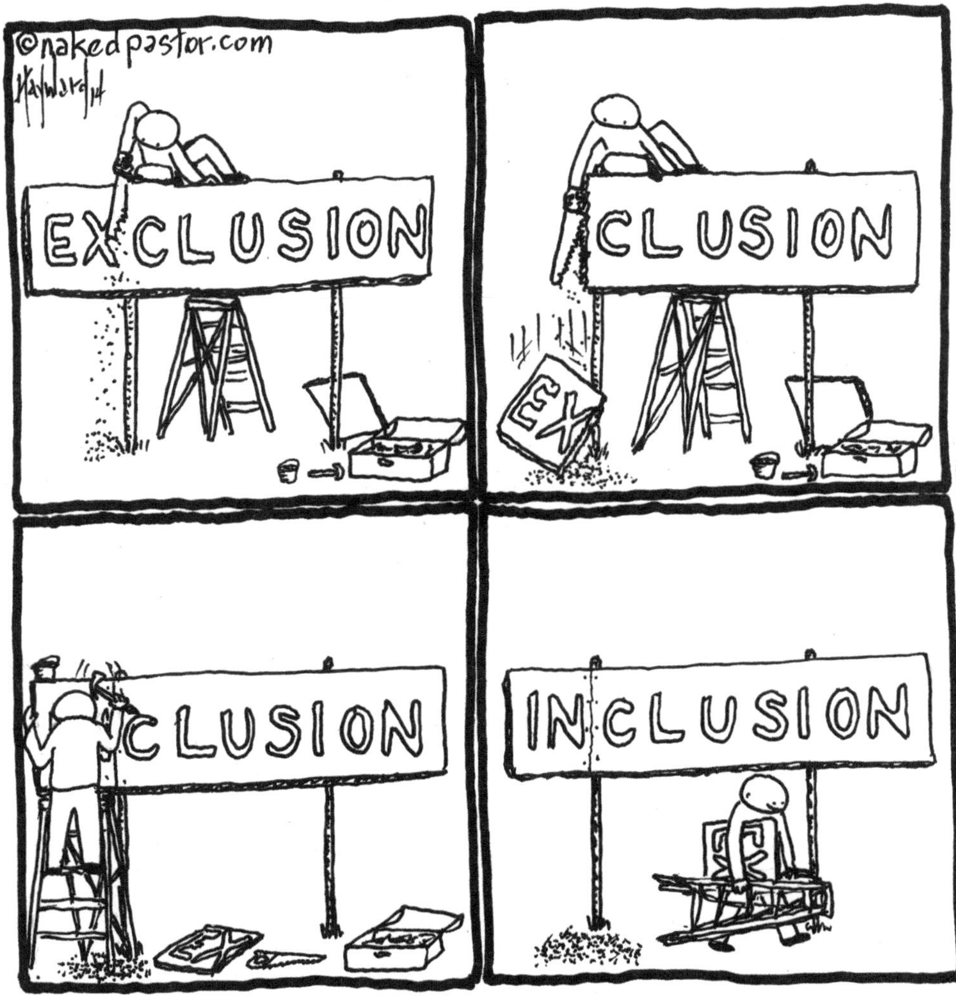
©nakedpastor.com
EXCLUSION
CLUSION
CLUSION
INCLUSION

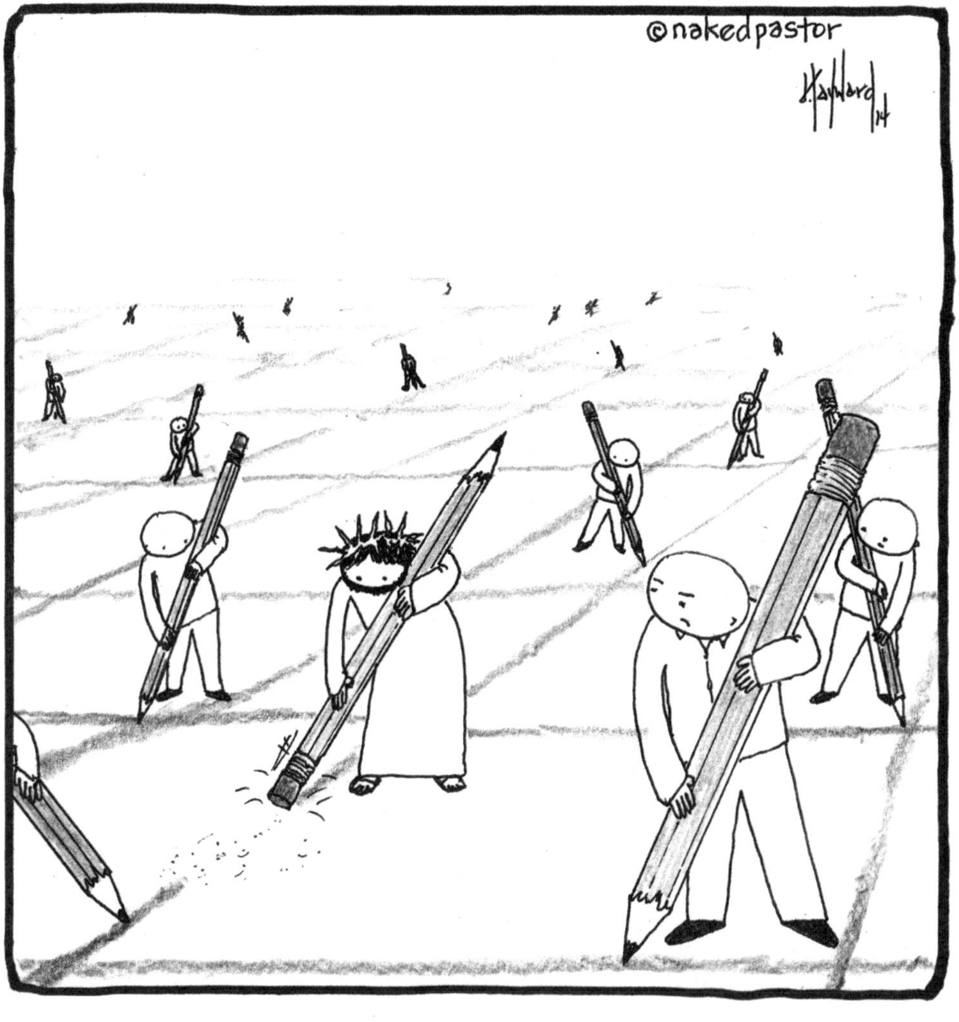
©nakedpastor
D.Hayward 14

ABOUT THE ARTIST

DAVID HAYWARD, who draws and writes as @nakedpastor, reaches wide audiences with fanciful and hard-hitting cartoons about spiritual abuse, the church's exclusion of LGBTQ+ people, faith and doubt, and feminism. With degrees from Gordon-Conwell Theological Seminary in South Hamilton, Massachusetts, and McGill University in Montreal, Hayward served as a pastor for most of his career, but in 2010 he left the professional paid clergy. His cartoons and other artwork have found their way all around the world. He and his wife, Lisa, who live near Saint John, New Brunswick, have three grown children.

Website: nakedpastor.com
Instagram: @nakedpastor
Facebook: @nakedpastor
Twitter: @nakedpastor
Pinterest: @nakedpastor
YouTube: youtube.com/user/nakedpastor

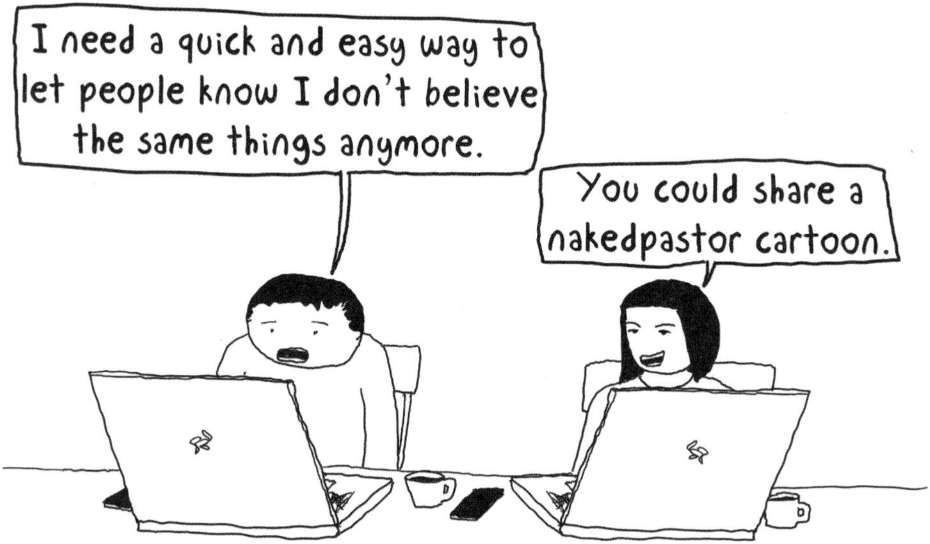
I need a quick and easy way to let people know I don't believe the same things anymore.
You could share a nakedpastor cartoon.